THE PMA EFFECT

How a Positive Mental Attitude can make you the badass you were born to be.

JOHN JOSEPH

Foreword by Rich Roll
Best-selling author of Finding Ultra

LOUD SPEAKER

Loudspeaker Publishing Company
32 Union Square East
New York, NY 10003

@2018 Loudspeaker Publishing Company

All rights reserved.

No part of this book may be reproduced in any form or by any means, electronic or mechanical, including photocopying, recording, or by any information storage or retrieval system, without permission in writing from the publisher.

PRINTED IN THE UNITED STATES OF AMERICA!

Distributed by MerchNow.

ISBN-13: 978-0-9983447-4-4

Back cover photo by Rob Mohr

"There is very little difference in people, but that little difference makes a big difference! The little difference is attitude. The big difference is whether it is *positive* or *negative*."

—*Napoleon Hill*

Table of Contents

FOREWORD... ix
INTRODUCTION... 1

PART ONE 9
   Positive Attitudes Are Forged in Fire.................... 11
   Get a Daily Practice 18
   Work That Farm.. 23
   Survive to Thrive 26
   Be All In 29
   Find a "Career," Not just a "Job" 31
   Let Passion Rule 34
   Never Minimize 42
   Accept Blame—Take Responsibility 44
   Develop Positive Friendships 47
   Start Small, Build Out, Get Your Shit Done 51
   Challenge Yourself Daily 55
   Have Integrity 60
   Earn Respect 62
   Set Goals and Visualize 65
   Look for a Mentor 69
   Each One Teach One 71
   Health Is Wealth—Stop Eating that Crap................. 75
   Exercise Like You Give a Fuck 84

PART TWO 89
Let's Dig Deep............................... 89
The Nature of the Mind: Thinking-Feeling-Willing 91
An Uncontrolled Mind Can Lead Us Right to Addiction..... 95
An Iron Will Manifests Through Discipline................ 99
Seize Opportunities 105
Become Resilient 112
You Must Turn Pro 117
Those Who Fail/Succeed 123
Simple Living & High Thinking 131
What Goes Around Comes Around................ 141
Act Like a Child 146
Find That Higher Power 151
Shhh... It's a *Secret* 156
A FREE Meditation Exercise—That's Right, FREE! 162
What Do You Mean, Happiness Is a Choice? 164
A Word on Grief 174
MRI for the Soul 179

PART THREE 185
Removing Stumbling Blocks 185
Don't Play the Victim—the Blame Game 187
Be Mindful of Criticizing Others 190
Never Procrastinate, Waste Time, or Give In to Resistance .. 192
OK, You Party Animals 196
What's with All the Complaining?.................... 200
Stop Stressing 203
Don't Identify with Negative Thoughts 212
Let Them Grudges Go........................ 216
Don't Hang Around With Negative, Unproductive People .. 219
Dating or Marrying the Wrong Person 222
Envy is Whack, So Stop Hating 226
The Four Disagreements 229

TABLE OF CONTENTS

PART FOUR 239
  Your Go-to Actions 239
  First Things First 241
  There Is No App For This 242
  Yo—Zip It!.. 247
  Risk and the Level of Reward 251
  Gratitude = Attitude 254
  They Ain't just Words 259
  Confidence Is the Cat 262
  When That Cheese Gets Moved...................... 266
  I Order You Fuckers To Laugh....................... 270
  Keep That Dream Alive 274
  My World... My Rituals 279
  Teamwork Works 282
  Reset Your Clock—Get Regulated 285
  Hit A Home Run Daily.................................. 290
  Learn From the Past 292
  Stay Bulletproof 294
  Invest in Sweat Equity 296
  See Adversity as a Blessing 299
  Your Mind Is Faster Than You Are................... 301
  Prioritize Your Goals................................... 304
  Change your World..................................... 307
  Take that Shot 311
  Have a Beautiful Obsession 313
  Wake Your Best Wolf 317
  Get PMA Fit 320
  Make Others Happy..................................... 322
  A Cause Bigger than Yourself 324
  Stay High Forever 328
  Fall in Love with Life 330
  Never Give Up 334
  Afterthoughts 337

  Acknowledgments 345

FOREWORD

John Joseph has an attitude problem.

But John's problem isn't his attitude. *It's yours.*

We all seek a better life. A life fueled by passion. A meaningful, purpose-driven life that jolts us out of bed in the morning and delivers our head to the pillow each night with an indelible feeling of gratitude, a profound sense of fulfillment, a deep connection with others and an absolutely undeniable sense of feeling truly alive.

This life isn't just possible, it's always within reach. Unfortunately, too few are equipped with the understanding, tools or discipline required to accomplish what is a very achievable end.

Why? Because our culture has perverted what is truly important. Because like sheep we have been duped to pray at the altar of false gods. From birth we are marketed to believe that our lives hold meaning only in relation to our ability to consume. That the value of personhood shall be calibrated in lockstep with the monetary value of our possessions. And so, as far back as we can remember, we function on the operating system of selfish material gain, mindlessly devoting our precious time and energy—*all told our lives*—to chasing the very things that do nothing but move us further away from the destination we most seek.

Perceiving the world as a zero-sum game, self-enrichment takes center stage as we measure ourselves against our peers. Security and comfort take precedence over challenge and sacrifice. Consumed with petty entitlement, we become frustrated and angered by others' success and ungrateful for what we already have. Focused solely on getting ours, we devote nary a thought for how we can benefit others.

Like entitled children, we spend the majority of our lives chasing what's ours without regard for what best serves our fellow man, our communities and the planet at large. Service is an inconvenient nuisance. Spirituality is antiquated and anti-intellectual. Meditation is an inconvenient annoyance. Friendships are for the unemployed. And asking for help is a display of weakness.

But when the happiness we seek eludes us, we fail to take personal responsibility for our actions and circumstances. Not once do we reflect upon ourselves. Not once do we turn that mirror upon ourselves. Not once do we take honest inventory for our choices, behavior and mindset.

Instead, we double down, deluded into the illusion that the contentment and meaning we desire will once and for all be delivered in the next job promotion, new car or relationship.

And when asked how we're doing, the most common refrain is, *I'm busy.*

Busy at what? Busy climbing a ladder that's leaning up against the wrong wall. Busy numbing ourselves from the pain of our daily grind. Busy getting busy. Busy pursuing everything and anything except that which will actually deliver on the promise of making us whole.

Busy-ness is big business. But it's merely a distraction that doesn't work. It never has and it never will. Because happiness is not a point system. It doesn't live in material accumulation. And it's not a destination that can be found outside ourselves.

Instead, happiness is a mindset. The love child of choice and action, it requires mastery over self—or what I like to call, the *warrior's path.*

Because we are so pre-conditioned to avoid risk and discomfort, most people aren't up for the challenge. Because it's easier to point fingers than take personal responsibility for our lives, we'd rather blame others for our dissatisfaction than undertake the risk, rigor, and self-reflection required to live our lives fully.

The result is always the same: depression, bitterness and victimhood. If you think I'm being hyperbolic, open your eyes. Never before in the history of humanity have we been fatter, lazier, sicker, more stressed or anxious. Right now, we are experiencing an unprecedented epidemic of obesity, heart disease, diabetes, cancer, mental illness, drug addiction, and many other chronic lifestyle illnesses—modern-day plagues that are unnecessarily killing millions of people every year.

To cope, we self-medicate, numbing and distracting ourselves with the very things that cause the problem in the first place: booze, pills, junk food, work, television, or our phones. In fact, we will fiendishly covet anything and everything to sidetrack us from confronting the uncomfortable truth of what truly ails us: a profound spiritual bankruptcy—a disease of self-seeking that isolates us from others, alienates us from the best part of ourselves, distances us from the healthy, fulfilling lives we so desperately seek, and ultimately crushes everything beautiful about what it means to be human and alive.

And this, my friends, is the root of John Joseph's attitude problem.

Because we need not suffer from this delusion. Both John and I are here to say that a happy, healthy life driven by passion and underscored by purpose is available to you if you are willing to let go of everything you thought you knew about what will get you there. Because chances are, everything you have ever been told about what it means to be truly successful in life is flat out wrong. It has nothing to do with your social status, your bank account, what kind of car you drive or the size of your home. Instead, it has everything to do with your relationship with yourself and others. It's about your willingness to engage adversity and weather failure. And it's about approaching life from a perspective of what you can contribute as opposed to what you can extract.

All told, it's about mindset and it's about character.

Breaking the chains of modern enslavement may require you to re-evaluate every aspect of your life from top to bottom. It's not easy. Perhaps it's the hardest thing you will ever do. But not only is it the most important work of your life, it's what you were born to do.

And it all starts with PMA—*positive mental attitude.*

It may sound trite. Every instinct you have may be working to dismiss this idea as cheesy. Too simplistic. Maybe even downright fucking stupid. But before you close this book and return to your lackluster, prosaic life, consider this: most of us are victims of an un-mastered mind. We fail to understand the vastness of consciousness. And that our brains are but tools that can be trained, just as our muscles.

This book is your call to action. A call to once and for all to stop living reactively. Because the salvation you seek has nothing to do with money, power or fame and everything to do with how you choose to engage the terrain of consciousness. In truth, the answers you seek lie dormant within. In fact, they have always been there, awaiting expression. The path forward is to tap into that inner power. To connect with what makes you uniquely you. And to breathe life into your unique blueprint and express the best, most authentic version of yourself for the benefit of others.

The survivor of a horrific upbringing, nobody would fault John Joseph for playing the victim card. What he endured would have buried most men. But John didn't just survive, he emerged victorious. Today he celebrates his life by giving back, selflessly devoting the best part of himself for the benefit of others less fortunate. His example is as instructive as it is inspirational.

Case in point: I never visit New York City without making sure to spend quality time with John. One of my favorite things to do with him is simply take a walk through his beloved Lower East Side neighborhood—ground zero for the horrific abuse that defined his life daily for decades. And yet it's impossible to walk more than 10 feet without John generously engaging strangers on the street in friendly conversation. He goes out of his way to check on every homeless person, providing food and loose change at will. And he considers every shopkeeper a family member, calling them by name and inquiring into the well-being of their loved ones. In truth, I have never met anyone more genuinely connected to his community, or more giving and concerned for others. In turn, John is one of the happiest, most positive, most productive, most fulfilled and beloved people I know.

This is not a coincidence. It is the direct result of a disciplined mind. A profound spiritual connection with something greater than self. An appreciation for our vast collective consciousness. And a deep understanding that a life of service is a life well lived.

This is true wealth. And by that logic, John is one of the richest men I know, fueled by a PMA that gives his life the kind of meaning, purpose, fulfillment and happiness we all seek.

This book is the roadmap to get you there.

So take John Joseph's hand.

Let him lead the way.

And then get to work creating a foundation for a new life. A life that very well may exceed that of your wildest imagination. I am proof. John is proof. And now it's your turn.

Because you deserve it. And now, more than ever, the world needs you to be more of who you really are.

PMA!

— **Rich Roll**
June 5, 2018

INTRODUCTION

As of late, people have been getting the letters PMA tattooed. I've also seen it on bumper stickers. Even the hit TV series *Breaking Bad* dropped a PMA reference. As for me, I'm bold enough to say these three letters can save your life.

If you ask those who have overcome tremendous adversity and gone on to win at monumental challenges, you'll see that the primary factor of their success is—and I guarantee you they will all give the same answer—developing and, more importantly, maintaining, a positive mental attitude throughout. PMA.

See, that's what separates the people who get their shit done from the ones who quit, who cave when adversity strikes. Everyone faces challenges in life. The real issue is how you deal with them. Point blank, if you don't harness the power of the mind you'll come up short in any endeavor that requires substance. The first step in harnessing the mind's power is to grasp its nature—to understand how the mind works and that the mind's a tool you can use to get to amazing places. Realizing the mind's potential by applying a certain set of methods is exactly what this book will do for you.

Now, let's get this out of the way right now, because I am not one to bullshit you. The path is difficult, as is anything of substance, but if you're willing to work, to shed some blood, sweat, and tears when you're tested, you'll get there. Successful people have no illusions about what's required. They know life's no cakewalk. But they maintain a positive state of mind and use the tools they're given.

So this book is *not* for those who always want to play it safe, who are never willing to take risks to get what they want. It's for those who know that anything of real value is dependent on the amount of risk you're willing to take to achieve it. The more something's worth, the greater the risk, if you don't have the proper mindset—without PMA—the faster you'll find yourself waving the white flag before you ever see the finish line. Seriously, think about the times you gave up on something difficult and analyze why. Nine times out of ten it was the voice in your head conning and deceiving you. That's what I refer to throughout this book as *The Enemy Mind*.

We've all spent countless years with our bad habits. We aren't going to change those habits overnight. Change takes patience and determination—it's not a sprint but a marathon. Actually, one of the cheapest tricks the disease called "resistance" uses to get you to quit in our instant, microwave society is to teach you to expect immediate results. I mean, sure, you'll see positive changes even in the beginning. But the real change? That takes time, and you'll have to put the work in every damn day.

Also, you should know that you'll be tested. The thing is to be able to identify your challenges as tests, work through them, and then move on. Understand that God, Krishna, Allah, Buddha, the Universe, or whatever you want to call your Higher Power, isn't picking on you. Rather, you're being pushed. And that push is the only way you can advance as a human being capable of accomplishing amazing things.

Do you think Michelangelo wasn't tested while painting the Sistine Chapel? He actually wrote a poem about the misery he endured while on that scaffold during those four agonizing years of his life: "My stomach's squashed under my chin, my face makes a fine floor for droppings, my skin hangs loose below me, my spine's all knotted from folding myself over." Yeah, he bitched, but he sucked it up and finished. He succeeded because he beat his mind with a stick every day, because that's how often the tests come.

Over the years I've read countless books, studied endless philosophy, met with scores of enlightened people—shit, I even lived as a monk for a few years just to be "all about it," as we say on the streets of New York. What I've learned is that the mind can be our best friend or our worst enemy. It's a tool in our toolbelt—no different from a knife or a screwdriver. It all comes down to bringing that tool under control and using it properly.

The process I've developed to do that comes from a lifetime of classes in the school of hard knocks and a decades-long search for truth, knowledge, and wisdom. I've presented the results in *The PMA Effect*. These methods are tried and true. Some of them date back tens of thousands of years to India's ancient yoga systems. Some are personal life lessons. Others come from persons who have, like many of us, overcome tremendous adversity and achieved amazing things in their lives. The bottom line, though, is that no book on self-improvement will benefit us if we don't apply what's contained in its pages. So apply the methods of *The PMA Effect* in your daily lives if you want to experience their benefit.

I was born in 1962 and have been around the block a few times—I've actually managed to learn a few things. First and foremost, we're in this world together. If we help one another, we can change the energy on the planet from the condition it's in now to one of immense unity, love, and compassion. That will only happen if we work on ourselves first. It makes no sense for us to jump off the boat to save someone who is drowning if we ourselves can't swim. That'll just make it two bodies to be fished out of the water.

Secondly, we must always remain ready to accept new ways of doing things, never thinking for a moment that we have all the answers. Personally, I'm still learning and trying to improve. I'm a work in progress, a neophyte on the path. But it's a path I'm happy to pursue daily and share with others as a way to pay forward the gifts I've received. The fact is, if people didn't snatch me from the turbulent waters of my own life, I'd either be dead or in jail. That's not some cliché bullshit story, either, my friends. That's real talk from a real New Yorker who was raised out on the mean streets. And yes, I'm still being tested daily, and yes I'm still reaching out to those who inspire and lead by their examples.

Which brings me to the writing of this book: as a result of the events in my life, I've had to apply everything I've learned over the years just to survive and stay on the path. I began to see a roadmap out of the mental hells we create for ourselves when our vision needs correcting. It's as if we have cataracts and, until they're removed, we can't see things clearly. The only way to remove them is through constant work and then applying what we've learned. You have to understand that life is all about being tested. You see, that's the checks-and-balances system to weed out posers, talkers, flappers, and wannabes—and keep them out of the way of the real-deal motherfuckers who get their shit done under any and all circumstances.

And mark my words, any time you try to break free from the status quo, to run from the herd, to separate yourself from those living out their quiet lives of desperation, to want more out of your time on earth, there will be many who mock and criticize you. Some will even become angry at what you're doing. Let them. Just go on being your badass self. I can't even tell you how many people, even so-called friends, tried to tell me I couldn't achieve the things I've accomplished. I never choose to believe that poison.

Science fiction writer Arthur C. Clarke, repeating wisdom that had been kicking around for hundreds of years, said, "Every revolutionary idea seems to evoke three stages of reaction. They may be summed up by the phrases: (1) It's completely impossible. (2) It's possible, but it's not worth doing. (3) I said it was a good idea all along." Remember that when you begin work on your improvement and you're called a new-age dipshit or when people say things like, "What, now you think you're better than everyone else? Fuck you." Finally, if they're at all honest, they too will take a look in the mirror as you and I have and admit they don't like the person standing there. When that happens, they'll start their own processes.

Finally, I made it through the things I did because I had ammunition in the form of knowledge, which I could take shelter of in my darkest hours. For that I thank my guru A. C. Bhaktivedanta Swami Prabhupada, the sages of Vedic philosophy, the warriors, my friends who always made time for me, those who consider me their enemy and have acted accordingly (for in the tests they've created for me I have grown immensely). But everyone has taught me valuable life lessons, without which none of this would be possible. It's from that place I humbly write this book and truly hope that you too find what's contained in its pages as useful as I have.

I've broken *The PMA Effect* into four parts. Each is integral to the process of developing and maintaining PMA. Like our four limbs, each serves the body as a whole. A severed arm or leg is of no use, so don't cut corners. Make a deal with me right here, right now, to do everything—all of it. If you do that, then like tens of thousands of people before you, I guarantee that you will become the badass you came to earth to be.

PART ONE

Every Journey Has a Starting Point

Let's get rolling by putting a strong foundation in place. We build from the ground up. Remember, change can only take place by actively applying what we learn.

Positive Attitudes Are Forged in Fire

Let me tell you a story about a kid who grew up in some of the worst circumstances imaginable.

As a young child he had to watch his mother get punched around by his father, who was a prizefighter-turned-alcoholic. At a young age, he and his two brothers were taken away from that mother and placed in an orphanage, followed by an abusive foster home, where the worst imaginable things happened for nearly seven years.

Finally, the State of New York's social worker got wind of what was going on and had the state shut the foster home down. He was then placed at Saint John's Home for Boys in Rockaway Beach. After a few months of that he ran into the freezing winter of January 1977 and hit the mean streets at a time when the city was one of the most violent places on earth. He survived by muling heroin, hustling angel dust, pills, and weed, as well as by breaking into stores and people's homes and stealing what he needed.

As a teen on the streets of NYC he was shot, stabbed, beaten, and also returned the favor of a good beating on more than a few occasions. He was completely alone, sleeping wherever he could in some of the most horrific conditions.

Well, as it happened, the law caught up to him and he was sent to the notorious Spofford Correctional Center in the Bronx, where he fought daily, being the only white kid in the entire facility. Then he was sent to another lockup north of the city, serving just under two years. When he got out, he joined the Navy and screwed that up. He was out of control, addicted to drugs and alcohol, extremely violent, and even smuggled and sold drugs while in uniform. (He was busted for that by undercover Narcotics Officers in Norfolk.)

Back in a jail cell, in a moment of self-reflection he wondered if God had cursed him to die an early death. I mean, why was all of this happening to him? That's when he had his "event,"—many people have similar "events" when they finally decide to stop playing the blame game and face the fact that it's time to man up and accept responsibility for their actions. Having it rough as a kid doesn't give you the right to do whatever you want to do. For this white kid, only he could change the road he was on.

It happened one day while driving around Norfolk, Virginia, where he was stationed in the spring of 1980. He passed a sign at a club called The Taj Mahal that announced "punk night." He pulled over, went inside, and stumbled on an amazing band that completely blew his shit away. After the show he met the singer, who talked about one song in particular and this thing called PMA. When he asked what PMA meant, he was told that no matter what we go through in life, we can get through it as long as we have a Positive Mental Attitude. Those words resonated deeply with him.

Well, as some of you know, that kid was me, the singer was HR, the band was the Bad Brains, and the song was "Attitude." HR copped the PMA philosophy off Napoleon Hill, who was one of the earliest authors to pen books on personal success—books like *Success Through a Positive Mental Attitude, Think and Grow Rich,* as well as one of my favorites, *The Law of Success,* where he talks about the Seventeen Principles of Success, PMA being one of them. In that book he writes, "Your mental attitude is the medium by which you can balance your life and your relationships to people and circumstances—to attract what you desire." Some of his other principles include being definite in one's purpose, maintaining sound health, teamwork, learning from adversity and defeat, going the extra mile, having a pleasing personality, and enthusiasm.

I practice a number of those principles every day, but I feel the basis of all my work on self-improvement began with having a positive mental attitude. Although it's been a long, hard battle, I wouldn't trade the struggle for anything in the world. Matter of fact, I still fight every day to stay positive, because I am fully aware that the alternative is a deep, dark, shithole that I never want to visit again.

Some people say that when you hit rock bottom you can only go up from there. That's bullshit. You can *always* fall lower. You can climb under the rocks with the worms and maggots and decaying carcasses; you can climb right into the shit, the muck, the scum, right down to a proverbial hell on earth. Unless, of course, you are willing to change.

Well, I sure as hell was. I needed to, because I knew if I didn't I wouldn't be around much longer. I knew where my train wreck of a life was headed. As badass as I thought I was, underneath the public mask, when I reflected on what was to come if I continued on my path of self-destruction, it truly scared the living shit out of me.

Many of you reading this know exactly what I'm talking about. We all have a journey, and although no two people are the same, I'm sure you can identify with what I'm saying because you may be in some of those places right now or know someone who is. Well, I can guarantee you with 100 percent certainty that positive change will come if you're willing to fight for it. I'm not going to sugarcoat this with a whole bunch of new-age, mumbo-jumbo bullshit about your aura or whatever. I'm NOT that guy. I'm the guy that's here to tell you straight the fuck up that you have to fight like hell, as if your life depended on it, because in all honesty it does.

This process of developing PMA has worked for me as well as some of the most highly-motivated, successful, badass people on the planet. I picked their brains to find out what makes them tick, how they got through shit, and what I found was that they all possessed one very important quality: they kept a positive mindset no matter what was going down.

So the choice is yours. You can decide to get with the program and see things in life as part of your growth even when they appear to be a chain of negative events. Or you can choose to live in a world where you are the victim, where your shortcomings and failures are everyone else's fault, where rather than rolling with that PMA you choose to live in a world of perpetual PMS. And yeah, guys, you can get that too. Matter of fact, I've had to stuff more than a few tampons down some D-bag's throat who made the mistake of bringing their crap into my area.

PMA is much more than a tattoo or a phrase we throw around because it sounds cool. It's something that can change your entire life. It can open doors to incredible places and new dimensions and relationships to things you never imagined possible. It all begins with the attitude you walk around with, the energy you put out in the world. Because it will attract a particular type of energy back to your life. That ain't some smelly, Birkenstock-wearing, hippie shit either. It's coming from someone who because of my stubbornness had to keep learning in the school of hard knocks.

So PMA, in essence, comes down to how we deal with life. How do you react to tough situations? Do you fly off the handle when the pressure's on or stop, take inventory, assess the situation, and figure out the best way to move forward?

Here's an example. As a young man I was angry and extremely violent because of the abuse I had suffered as a child. I lashed out at everyone around me. I self-medicated with drugs and alcohol and never looked for a way out of my suffering. That nearly cost me my life. Then, as I started taking an internal inventory, I found myself beginning to heal. Day by day I put what I was learning into practice, and bit by bit I turned the corner on all my bad shit.

I'm not special. That's what it takes for everyone—rolling up your sleeves and getting dirty, never taking shortcuts. That's how you pull yourself out of the crap and work toward achieving a positive mindset. Every day you have to monitor the ebb and flow of your thoughts, desires, and actions and question where they will get you in terms of reaching your goals.

Fire can be an all-consuming force that burns everything to the ground, or it can be used to forge a sword to help you cut through ignorance and *maya* (illusion). You can use fire to help you see things for what they are, to gain perspective. Like fire on a blacksmith's forge, fire forges our character. It does so through burning—challenging—us. Your true character is only revealed under pressure. The greater the pressure, the greater the revelation.

We're all trying to make our way in the world and be happy. In order to succeed at happiness, we *must* find out what we're made of. There's no half-stepping with that. You must challenge and invest in yourself. Welcome life's tests and be prepared to enter the battlefield, ready to fight under any and all circumstances, to cut down the three great enemies: negativity, self-doubt, and resistance. The only way to win this war is to remain steadfast and determined, to fight to the end. Enter the battle with the greatest weapon in your arsenal: your PMA sword.

Get a Daily Practice

Pay attention here, because what you're about to read is one of the most important aspects of this book.

Despite how much work I've done on myself, or what I've been able to overcome and achieve, if I don't have a positive foundation in place through a daily *sadhana* (meditation/spiritual) practice, my mind can and will lead me to negative places in the material world. *Sadhana* is your coat of armor against bad vibes.

I learned this when I was living a monk's life. Every morning we were up at 2 a.m.—no time for bullshit. Every minute of every day used properly, aimed at growth. That's exactly why you need a daily practice. A regimen. Whether it's yoga, meditation, a swim, a workout, maybe just five minutes of mindfulness in your busy day, use it to look inward and take inventory. Trust me on this, it will pay huge dividends.

That's why when people look to me for help, the first thing I do is some troubleshooting. I ask, "Okay, Joe, what's your program?" They use that term in lockup. I was asked that same question when I went to those maximum security prisons for Scared Straight in the 1970s. The Lifers Group members asked me what I was doing each day to better myself while I was still locked up. Ask me? Shit, they screamed it in my face. But I had no answer.

For us it's a little different, but the essence is the same: what internal work are you doing each day to better yourself? If the answer is nothing, therein lies the root of your troubles. If I start working on a huge calculus problem but start with 2+2 = 5, then everything else will be wrong. It doesn't matter how many hours it takes me, all my work is useless.

So get with the program. If you don't have one, make one. There's no one-size-fits-all *sadhana*. What works for me won't necessarily work for you. But you'll find your path by seeking it and taking action. That's how you figure things out. Not by hypothesizing or speculating, trying to taste that sweet maple syrup by licking the outside of the jar. You have to crack that bad boy open. That's how life works.

It's said that practice makes perfect. True. Perfection in human life is 100 percent attainable. To seek perfection is why we're in human bodies. As humans we have every gift at our disposal. People who say otherwise are fools. Now, is it easy? Hell, no. Nothing of great value is. But perfection can be attained if we overcome the **Four Defects**—the tendency to cheat; the tendency to make mistakes; the tendency to fall under the spell of illusion (*maya*); and the fact that our senses are imperfect. These defects are causing us trouble. But all four can be cured by doing intense, internal work—something confirmed by India's ancient Vedic literature, by gurus, and by other enlightened beings.

Enlightened beings, wisdom literature, and realized spiritual teachers (gurus) provide the checks-and-balances system that helps us keep straight. I don't give two shits about what atheists say as they deny the existence of God. They've never opened the jar of maple syrup to taste what's inside. Instead, they've only speculated or denied that maple syrup *can* be sweet (or exists at all). Anyone who has actually tasted maple syrup knows what I'm talking about. Their denial is called frog-in-the-well philosophy. Please allow me to elaborate.

One day, a frog leaves his well and goes out to see the sights, finally finding himself on the shore of the Pacific Ocean. On his return he tells the other frogs in the well—none of whom have ever left the well—about the great body of water he's just seen. The other frogs want to know how big the ocean is, so they start trying to compare their well to the ocean. "Is it three times the size of our well?" The traveling frog says, "No, no, it's much, much larger. Go see it for yourself. Then you'll know what a wonder it is!" But his friends don't want to leave the well, so they continue their line of questioning, "Is it four times bigger? Twenty times? A hundred times the size of our well?" All the while the more adventurous frog tells them to just take action—leave the well and have the same experience he did. But no, they'd rather stay where they are, speculate, and deny that there could ever be a body of water bigger than something they can compare to the one they know.

You get the point. Don't be like those frogs. Find your practice and dive into the ocean. Discovering my *sadhana* was crucial for my development, but I had to work out a lot of kinks in it and in myself. I've also monitored the *sadhanas* of others I've known for decades—not to judge them but to learn. I like to observe people. That's why when people say things like "The years haven't been good to him/her" I know that more than likely it's because that individual hasn't been good to him or herself.

> **The key to developing *sadhana* is consistency. Consistency's how you get good at anything—martial arts, yoga, swimming, running, writing... and especially at keeping your PMA. You have to show up constantly, *especially* on the days you don't want to.**

Lately, I've been practicing the Wim Hof Method of breathing. I do it in the morning, but sometimes I feel like, "I'll do it later." That's a trick of the Enemy Mind. You know as well as I do that nine times out of ten you will NOT get to it later. When I put things off that I made a deal with myself to do, I feel like shit because I gave in to resistance. On the flip side, after I do my breath work and practice my mindfulness and meditation, I feel I can accomplish anything. That's because all energy flows from that higher place—the spiritual center that is our essence. Every one of us are part and parcel of that higher spirtual nature. That's what unites us—all of us. When you're united you don't look at others and judge them based on their material coverings (bodies) but see everyone as equals at that very basic, spiritual level. Imagine how fast we could fix the planet if we all worked out from there.

PMA is an investment in yourself, and you better your chances of attaining it if you practice. So in the beginning, take baby steps if that's all you can do. At least you'll have a starting point. Just try to invest in yourself by putting something into your internal bank account every day. It may be that your schedule on a particular day only allows you five minutes to meditate, do some breathing exercises, a little yoga, or maybe even read some philosophy. The point is, when you do your practice daily—when you make that effort—it pays dividends in the form of letting you begin to turn the corner on some of your problems. Just keep chipping away day by day and always work from the inside out.

Work That Farm

One of the things I do is take an inventory of how I spend my time. Time is our greatest commodity, and all the money in the world can't buy back even one millisecond of it.

That's why I ask, "What will these particular thoughts, words, or actions do for me and how will they get me to where I want to be?" And if I realize I'm going nowhere, I stop those particular thoughts, words, or actions and change course.

You're shaping your future right now. You've planted a seed of PMA just by picking up this book. Every day you're either planting seeds that will produce fruits of positivity or planting weeds that'll choke the life out of your fragile PMA seedling. This farmer analogy is great when trying to understand this. Let's take a look at it.

An organic farmer readies his soil by plowing. Turning the soil over increases the soil's oxygen content and kills the fast-growing weeds that can crowd out the desired crop by competing for water and essential nutrients. Next, he adds organic fertilizer to the soil—essential for plant growth because it makes more oxygen available for the plants' roots. Then, and only when the soil temperature is right for seed germination, does he plant his seeds. Then during the growing season he makes sure the field has sufficient water and nutrients.

Think of plowing as our daily positive thoughts and actions. Positivity gives the vitality we need in our lives in order to grow. Positive thoughts tend to uproot negative emotions—the weeds in our analogy—or prevent them from taking root. The fertilizer is the company we keep; good, positive farmers who themselves have raised or are trying to raise a PMA crop feed us the knowledge and support we need to raise our own PMA crop. Watching them and their process can prepare us for the road ahead. We know that timing is everything, so waiting for the temperature to be right requires patience. And when it's right, it requires action—planting your seeds. So make sure you're well prepared for any of life's tasks. Once you've planted your PMA seeds and whatever companion plants you need to support it, keep your field sufficiently watered by filling your days and nights with activities that give you a sense of well-being. Those actions should be of a positive nature, obviously, and not things that drag down your consciousness.

Reading this book and applying what's in here means planting seeds and farming for your future. You'll have positive yields as long as you plow, weed, fertilize, watch your ecology, act when the time is right, and keep your crops watered. It's not by accident that I'm putting this practice section right up front. As I said earlier, you can read all the books you want on self-improvement, but if you don't apply what they teach you'll be like a farmer who stares at his field, never works it, but expects, by some miracle, that he'll get a healthy crop.

It's imperative that you make your best effort. You know when you half-ass something, when you don't work properly, so don't. Always ask yourself, "What do I want my future to look like?"

People who get shit done are not resting on past laurels; they're constantly trying to improve themselves and their situation by acting. They're constantly planting new seeds. Last year's harvest doesn't matter. What matters is today's and how we want our future crops to turn out. Don't let weeds take root and don't waste time. Get out there, bust your ass, and work that field.

Survive to Thrive

"Every day above ground is a good day, Johnny." You know who told me that? A friend who survived time in prison, spent decades addicted to drugs, and was almost murdered on several occasions.

This kid had one tough paper route, as they say. When he did finally kick the bad shit to the curb—well, I've never met a more positive person in my life. Every morning he got to open his eyes and see the sunrise he considered it a blessing. He survived a *ton* of bad shit, and with the gift of his new life he made damn sure he used his time on earth to push himself, to try and be better than he had been the day before.

I saw a post today on Facebook: "It's okay if all you did today was survive." I get that. You're not going to have a huge breakthrough every day. If you think that you are, you're sadly mistaken and setting yourself up for a letdown. Life is ebb and flow. You're going to have good days and bad ones. Take them in stride. Appreciate every day. Learn to survive; then you'll figure out how to thrive.

Every day for the last thirty-six-plus years, the first thing I do when I wake up is touch my head to the floor and say my mantras. I give thanks for the gift of life. For all the tests that brought me to where I am. It starts my day off right. It's a mindset, you know, this whole PMA thing. You develop it slowly, day by day, as year after year you grind out each and every win against adversity.

Now, just imagine for a second how someone who just survived a near-death experience treats the following day, how she watches the sunrise, breathes air, looks at the trees, watches the birds, acts toward others. She doesn't take any of it for granted, that's for sure. We have to look at each and every day in exactly the same way: as a gift.

Have you ever watched those nature shows where caribou have to cross a river filled with crocodiles? Them caribou ain't fucking playin'. Their instinct and will to live pushes them to do whatever it takes to make it to another day. Those who are passionate about doing positive shit don't need to be forced to act on it either. Through practice, PMA becomes instinctual. They can't wait to get at a new day. They welcome life's challenges because they're aware that challenges only make them stronger.

Now, on the other side of the coin are those who get a jolt or jolly from being negative—by being an asshole to people or talking smack or finding fault. I know people who live for that shit. That type of energy won't sustain them. It's limited. History has proven this fact time and again. In the end, positive wins over negative every time, and that's why you have to walk with PMA.

Have the mindset to be thankful for the fact that you've been given another day on the planet to fulfill your dreams. Do everything in your power to make those dreams a reality.

That won't happen if you get caught up in petty bullshit with petty-minded people. My boy who went through all that told me straight up, "I got no time for drama. I had decades of wasting my time with it. I'm trying to get somewhere now."

Be All In

When people tell me shit's not going the way they want in life I always ask them how much of themselves they've invested in what they're trying to accomplish, regardless of what that may be—building a career, bettering a relationship, getting fit, whatever.

If it's not 100 percent, I tell them straight up that they got no right to complain. I see this a lot with people who move to New York City from other places to live out their hopes and dreams. I can't even tell you the number who pack up and move home.

A common denominator of most of them is that they didn't fully commit. They got caught up in the nightlife, the partying, maybe a destructive relationship or two, or any one of the other distractions a place like New York City can offer. I compare those distractions to the jewels on the head of a serpent. At first you're attracted by the razzle-dazzle, but as you get close, BAM! Death of desire, maybe even actual death. I've seen it happen to those who got caught up in drugs and alcohol.

> **That's why you have to be all in. You have to go after what you want. Remove the obstacles that hold you back from your dreams. Life is a high-stakes game—winner take all.**

Always remember, right now there is someone working his or her ass off to get that position at work you covet, that acting role you're preparing for, maybe the MMA fight, that qualifying spot in the Boston marathon or the Kona Ironman World Championship. There are hungry people out there, and hunger makes you one determined SOB. Believe me, I know. Starving as a kid in that foster home made me what I am today. Back then I had no choice in whether or not I could eat. Now, it's up to me. I never want to go back to that physical hunger, so every day I get up early and work my ass off. That way, I'm sure that when opportunity, timing, and luck meet, I'm prepared to take advantage. That's success, and it comes from engrossing yourself wholeheartedly in the work—whatever that work is. If I know one thing for sure it's this: without completely immersing your energy in the tasks in your life, you will never achieve the results you desire.

Find a "Career," Not just a "Job"
(but work your ass off until it comes)

A job is something you have to do to cover your bills. A career is something you love and would be willing to do even if you don't get paid. You simply love doing it.

Many struggle between career and job because the work you love really doesn't always pay or pay well enough. So we have to work for our maintenance, then do a double—go home and work on whatever it is we *really* want to be doing with our lives.

When we work hard and keep a positive mental attitude even when we're working our job—even when we don't want to be waiting tables or working construction—the muse recognizes our hard work and lends us a helping hand, bolstering our inspiration, creativity, or in some way providing opportunities to do more.

Then there are those who have the opposite mentality. I've met them countless times in New York City. I'm talking about those who work a job but do it with a shitty, stank-ass attitude. Think of the waiters who are texting and gabbing about their latest audition with their coworkers while your food sits cooling and the cook is ringing the bell for them to pick it up and give it to you. And God forbid you complain! If you do, they give you the gas face: "Man, fuck you. I ain't no waiter. I'm gonna be a famous actor." "Yeah, homie? Well, congratulations on that in advance, but for now you're my waiter, so go get me my fucking soup already before I drop a monologue on you that you're not gonna like."

Point blank, when you see people with an attitude like that at their job, I can guarantee with 100 percent certainty that it will carry over to their career. If they ever do manage to land a role, the director will likely throw their ass off his set.

I've always worked hard. I did double duty before my career ever started to pop. I was a bike messenger in NYC for ten years, riding in the worst weather and traffic insanity you can imagine, flying up and down streets, dodging cabbies, and doing it while living in an abandoned building on the Lower East Side. No running water or electricity, showering at a fire hydrant in the dead of winter, dealing with the violent drug dealers who were trying to take the building from those of us who lived there. I've also done twelve-hour construction shifts. With both jobs I've then gone home and banged out scenes for my script, penned words for a song, or wrote pages for my books. I have no patience for crybabies, whiney fucks, self-entitled trust-funders, or lazy bastards.

When I worked my jobs I did it with a smile. And with PMA. We all have bills to pay and need money. Work your ass off and then use every spare minute you have for your career. I'm still doing that. Shit, I recently painted a friend's apartment to make some cash, even though I have a major publishing deal on the front burner. I hustle and do whatever it takes when I'm working hard because I know I'm also putting the hours into my career.

I know we're not all meant to be writers, actors, or rock stars, but we're all something. So what I'm advocating here is to find that something—anything that you can be passionate about—even if it's a hobby that gives you a creative outlet. Don't just be a cog in the machine. That will crush your human spirit. When you create something you resonate with, you use all your potential, energy, and focus. That's why we feel so alive while we're doing it.

All the hard work I've done for decades is beginning to pay off career-wise, but to get to this point I had to push on and have PMA in my "jobs." PMA was an integral part of my process of self-development; the two go hand in hand. A shitty attitude will carry over into all aspects of your life, so be careful.

Let Passion Rule

A journalist recently interviewed me and asked, "So, John, we're all proactive and making things happen in our youth, but how do we keep that spirit and fire burning as we get older?"

My answer was simple. When we find something we're so passionate about that we can't wait for our feet to touch the floor in the morning so we can have at it, there's no question of that fire ever losing its blaze. Let passion drive you on. Such passion comes through showing up constantly to do the thing we love.

Webster's Dictionary defines *passion* as "a strong feeling of enthusiasm or excitement for something or about doing something." I like to think of it as an unrelenting, driving force that consumes you. As the great filmmaker Fellini said, "There is no end. There is no beginning. There is only the passion of life."

LET PASSION RULE

Some of the most positive people I've met have been the most passionate. That's not by accident. PMA is a by-product of passion, because when you find your calling and you're up every day going at it, you can't help but be positive.

Speaking from personal experience, when I started writing songs, books and film scripts, my days and nights were consumed with learning and applying the craft. I'd wake up, say my mantras, jump out of bed, do my pushups and sit-ups, make my juice, and then I'd be off to the lab—which in my case was the back room where I keep my computer and corkboard.

Honestly, getting into writing has saved me from so much unnecessary bullshit and drama. People would be like, "Yo, John, did you hear that so-and-so got into a bar fight last night and got stabbed?" "Nope. I was at home, writing." And loving it, I might add.

So many negative things in your life can be avoided by finding a positive passion, because passions force you to develop a positive mindset. And that forces you to block out the negative people you just don't have time for because you're too busy doing positive shit. Maybe it's joining a gym, eating healthy, training for a triathlon, doing a Tough Mudder, or heeding the philanthropic call to feed the homeless or build fresh-water wells in Africa or India—whatever it is, love it. Then you'll never let anything stop you from doing it.

I'm turning 56 this year (2018), and I'm more passionate and driven than ever to accomplish my goals. I have a number of goals: do an Ironman triathlon, write and publish this book, work on a movie or TV show. I even plan to raise the funds to open another bhakti yoga center that will provide free classes and feed the homeless organic, plant-based meals. But first, I had to envision and establish these goals. Writing them down and putting them up on my corkboard makes them real instead of shit-talk. Then I start small and build out. I finish one project and start another. There is no downtime. Life is too short for that.

Don't give the Enemy Mind a chance to rear its ugly head. It takes discipline to develop a strong work ethic, but it's a discipline we need in order to kick ass in life. You think Oprah didn't work her butt off to get where she is? Actually, I retweeted something she said yesterday: "Don't make excuses for why you can't get it done. Focus on all the reasons you must make it happen." Right on, sister.

I believe that people's callings will find them. First things first, though. Start by clearing away the negativity in your life. Negativity will make you stumble. Be ready when your passion comes calling. Preparing the ground for it is a process, a beautiful one, and it'll make you fall in love. That's not some new-age, cornball bullshit. I don't throw around words like *love* and *beautiful* cheaply. I mean, look where my life has taken me; from daily hell to daily happiness—to PMA. Why? Because I did the work. I let the passion and desire to accomplish my goals rule my days and nights. I took action and gave negative fuckers around me their walking papers. I just don't have time for negativity.

When I began my music career in 1981, the business was nothing like what you see today. We didn't have Youtube, Facebook, Instagram, Twitter, Spotify, Iphones, or the Internet. Hell, no. We had to work in the trenches. I did it with a smile on my face most of the time because I loved what I was doing. I starved, slept on people's floors, fought for my life and was broke. We played sold-out tours in clubs and arenas, then came back to NYC homeless, living in squats with no windows or running water because our manager was ripping us off. But every night I got to go on stage and do what I loved. That made it all worthwhile.

Music has been a saving grace throughout most of my life. The earliest memories I have of my mom, I was five years old and living in Queens. 1967. We lived in a rundown apartment, where we were going through hell on earth. My piece-of-shit father would roll up after not being around for weeks, push his way in, and beat the crap out of my mom, taking the only money she had to feed us with. I grew up with crazy violence. I've lived with crazy violence my entire life. Matter of fact, I didn't find out until I was forty that I'd been conceived through rape. My mother left her rapist's ass after my older brother was born, but he later broke in and beat and raped her. Since they were still legally married, the cops did nothing. He did the same thing a year later, and that's how my younger brother came into this world. Many, including her family, told my mother to get an abortion—who wants to carry a rape pregnancy to term? But I'm thankful she didn't listen to them and that she endured incredible adversity and made tremendous sacrifices. By the time she was twenty-one she had had three kids. She had no way to support us and still had to dodge her rapist's beatings.

But no matter what we were going through, as soon as she put those Motown 45s on in our living room, that world of pain disappeared. Me, my two brothers, and my mom would dance around, happy as hell. The music and the passion my mom had to provide for us and be a good mother is the only thing that got us through those early years before it became too much for her and depression took over.

Even when things got real ugly and the state took us away and placed us in an abusive foster home, where scumbag foster parents and their other kids tried to break my spirit, I lay under my blanket in that dirty garage that doubled as a bedroom with my little AM transistor radio playing the hits on WABC. Or I watched "Soul Train" on the little round TV with its clothes-hanger antenna and danced along with those "Soul Train" dancers. I'd enter a whole different world—one where life was beautiful and all the pain dissipated. I fantasized about being a singer, climbing into a slick, customized van and traveling the country with my brothers. I had no idea what touring even meant, but I just wanted to travel and play music. Those dreams helped me forget about everything that was happening to us.

It was the same thing on those cold nights, all alone on the streets of NYC in the mid-70s. Music filled the void. Jail? Music.

When I was living in those burned-out buildings in Alphabet City in the early '80s, Puerto Rican gang members trying to take our building at gunpoint, I still woke up every day, took a shower at the fire hydrant despite subzero temperatures, and got on my bike to messenger all day. Why? So I could pay for Cro-Mag rehearsals. I was the living, breathing embodiment of determination. And not because I had dreams of being a rock star. I just loved what I was doing, so I pushed on and endured. Music was one of the things that helped me kick drugs. It has always been music that pulled me out of the worst things life threw at me. Now do you see my point about passion and what you can accomplish when you find yours?

Sometimes I still find myself slacking off, not giving my all to a project—putting things off, telling myself I'll do it tomorrow. There *is* no tomorrow; there's only today. Procrastination is a tool in resistance's arsenal, and it's one that will drive us to eventually quit if we don't put the kibosh on it pronto.

Now, when you first read this book, you might think how deceptively simple it all seems, but when you actually set out and apply it to your life, you'll see how deep it actually is.

I'm telling you right here, right now: passion is a true gift and there's nothing more I want for any of you than to find your passion, because that passion will open to you a world of amazing gifts.

Perhaps this section will inspire some of you to push forward with passion and offer the world your amazing piece of literature, an album, or a film of great beauty, substance, and depth. Lord knows we need what you have to give.

My writing guru, Mr. Robert McKee, told me there's a direct correlation between the decline of values in society and a decline in the arts. Look at the condition of the arts today. All this dumbed-down, rock-star fantasy crap poisoning the youth. Reality TV stars with their photo-shopped asses filling the pages of magazines, their lives devoid of any type of higher consciousness. Or some jerk-off who's got guns and money telling you how he's the shit. It's all poison, free from any type of revolutionary thought. Cheap entertainment makes us all puppets of corrupt governments. That's why one tyrant said, "Kill the artists first. They are the freethinkers in society and the most dangerous."

The real messages are out there, though. They're just not in the mainstream. You have to look for them in the underground. Music and other forms of art make you freethinkers. Nowadays everyone is told to work like an ass in the factory or join the military to fight some overseas corporate war, to become robots incapable of thinking for themselves, controlled by the garbage lies the news media puts out. Slaves to consumerism. I'd like to think that most of you reading this are trying to make yourselves and the planet a better place, one we can leave for the next generations better than we found it.

So whatever your passion project is, push through and arm yourself with the knowledge of this book and others like The Four Agreements and Bhagavad Gita As It Is. Develop the determination that little John Joseph had and make a better life for yourself. See things through to the end. When I asked a member of the Bad Brains—a band that'd risen from dirt poor, from the ghetto streets of D.C., to become the most legendary punk bands on the planet—what drove him, he looked me dead in the eye and said, "I had to. What else I got?" 'Nuf said, Darryl.

So let me ask you, what's your passion? What are you here to give? What gift can you offer the planet that no one else can offer in quite the same way? What makes you jump out of bed in the morning? That thing you never get sick and tired of? That thing you get so engrossed in that you never want to stop? You find that, my friends, and you will be one happy, badass, motherfucking human.

Never Minimize

When you're facing a problem, instead of dealing with it do you tell yourself that it's insignificant? If you answered yes, be careful. You can only avoid problems for so long before you explode.

People have a tendency to ignore problems, such as issues with people, debt, disease, obesity, and so many other things. Don't. You need to take action and address your problems immediately.

If I have an issue with someone I deal with it head-on. It's the best way to do it. Don't hold a grudge—clear the air and your mind. Be tactful; don't be rude.

You'll feel much better, and you won't be stressed. If there's a health issue I do the same. No problem fixes itself. Letting a disease progress only intensifies the illness.

The one area people try to minimize is stress—they avoid dealing with what's causing it. But stress catches up to you. Small problems only become huge issues the longer we avoid them. When stress levels increase, it leads to debilitatated health, which leads to a negative mindset, not to mention the negative ways of dealing with stress—drinking, smoking, medication, over-or-under-eating, taking your stress out on others by letting your temper explode, to name just a few.

So don't take a back seat in your own life by minimizing things. You're the driver. Stay in the driver's seat and take charge. Deal with things when they come up. Some may not like the fact that I'm brutally honest and tell them when they piss me off or do some foul shit, but you know what? I don't care. I call it as I see it, and you should too. It's part of being impeccable with your word. More on that later.

I also appreciate when people tell me I'm screwing up, that I'm wrong. That's a real friend, not some kiss-ass who tells you you're the greatest thing since sliced bread. The fact is, if several people in your camp are telling you the same thing—that you're effen up—perhaps it's time for you to address it. Don't let small issues in any area of your life spiral out of control to become major problems. Always deal with them as soon as they arise.

Accept Blame— Take Responsibility

We live in a world of cause and effect, action and reaction. As such, life is about interactions with others. You do or say something to loved ones, people you work with, or Joe Schmo on the street, and there's a reaction to what you've said, favorable or otherwise.

Transferring blame instead of sitting back and analyzing the situation, perhaps accepting that you were wrong, means we don't have to fix ourselves. "Nah, man, fuck that. It's their fault."

Bullshit. That, my friends, is the quickest way to a negative mindset, because we constantly make ourselves victims instead of taking action that can direct a situation toward the positive. This is a principle that took me years to figure out, and I'm still dealing with it. As I said, I'm a work in progress. I'm not writing this as if I'm cured.

I learned a very important lesson from a yoga master: "Always take the humble position."

In other words, accept the blame that belongs to you. Put your pride and false ego aside.

If anything happened to that yoga master that brought negative reactions into his life, he never pointed the finger at others. Instead he simply said "It's my karma. Perhaps in this life or the last I treated someone in the exact same way, and so I've caused this." Man, that's some deep realization, let me tell you. I mean, take a fucker like me for example, who in the past has admittedly done grimy shit. Yet I'm still ready to blame the next guy when things happen. Then there's this dude, living the life of a saint and talking like that. Wow! It really made a lasting impression.

I see this a lot when people fail in their careers. Instead of accepting the fact that perhaps they could have done things differently, that maybe they were the one's who fucked up or that maybe they just didn't work hard enough, it's always the other people's fault because everybody's out to dog them. But oh, how we love the success when it finally comes. Then it's all our doing, right?

Look, if things aren't happening the way we want them to, it's no one else's fault but our own. We have to fix them. No one will do it for us, so stop passing the buck and playing the victim. Do the work and man up, as they say on the streets. That goes for you ladies as well.

Just sit back for a moment and imagine a world where everyone puts this principle into action—they all accept responsibility and look at themselves and their shortcomings instead of passing the buck and blaming others. If every man, woman, or spiritual or political leader took the humble position like that yoga master, we'd fix this planet's problems within twenty-four hours. The truth is, we can't worry about others. You don't control how others deal with things; you can only control yourself. So stop the blame game put this into practice in your daily life, and watch everything around you change for the positive.

Eventually, others around you will catch on, and if they don't—well, there's an old saying in India, "The dogs may bark, but the elephants must carry on." Just "do you" and don't get caught expecting things to always go your way: "Well, I was fucking humble and he/she still acted like a dick to me." First off, if you say you're humble, you ain't. Second, by expecting a particular result, more than likely you'll be let down. That's why you always have to act just for the sake of the act itself and not its result. It will change nothing if you develop the mindset of thinking you can always control the outcome of the things you do. You can't. So always take the humble position. Turn that mirror around and look at yourself before you pass the blame.

Develop Positive Friendships

Let me declare it boldly that 99.99 percent of any positive progress I've made in my life has been due to the people I've spent time with.

That also works in the opposite direction, you know, such as when I was fucking up bad. I mean, look at my story: I ran the streets, dealt drugs, and hung out with crazy maniacs. Where did that get me? In jail and addicted to drugs. Then in 1980 I met the Bad Brains and all the positive people surrounding them and voilà! PMA and change. Association is the key, and nothing will lift you out of a shit storm quicker than hanging around with positive and positively motivated people.

There are three classes of intelligence. First-class is when we hear, "Hey, don't touch the fire or you'll get burned" and that's sufficient—we heard, we listened, we learned, and there was no need to get burned. Second-class intelligence is to hear the warning not to touch the fire and then to touch it. We get burned, we learn. No need to repeat that mistake. We learned the hard way. Third-class intelligence means we touch the fire over and over. We don't learn from instructions or our own experience.

Personally, I've always fallen somewhere between second- and third-class intelligence. Perfect example: even after I learned a lot in the early '80s by associating with a drug addict, in '88, after my so-called best friend and bandmate robbed the band, I quit the Cro-Mags and again became deeply addicted to drugs. I smoked crack, drank alcohol, took pills, and was almost murdered several times. I kept going back to touch that flame and I got burned again and again.

That's why I'm now very careful about who I spend time with. My associates are all first-class intelligence types, and after nearly three decades of good association I'm slowly moving toward that as well. Again, it's a process.

> **You can't expect overnight success because it doesn't work that way. We are so hard-headed and stuck in our ways, our conditioning runs so deep, that it just takes time to change— perhaps even an entire lifetime.**

But we must gain access to *sadhus*—people with first-class intelligence and knowledge in order to cut the ropes of our own ignorance. Actually, the Sanskrit word *sadhu* literally means "one who cuts." But even after we gain access to good association, it's still up to us to act on the knowledge they offer. Remember, there are no armchair philosophers allowed on the PMA path. You must *do your work*.

The hard truth is that we have to be a little selfish with our time on earth because it's limited. It's not that I'm better than anyone else, trust me. Far from it. The thing is, I have so much work to do on myself that I'd rather be around those who can either impart knowledge to me or teach me by example. Those who set the example are the ones I can learn best from.

That's why I've had to start avoiding people who constantly approach me with the same damn problems, but who, when it's time to take action, make excuses and go get high or drunk. Look, I'm all for helping others, but not by dragging them out of a bar at three in the morning or some crack spot. (Shit, are those fucking things even around anymore?)

The point is, we have to establish, build, and maintain positive association and friendships. Then when we have issues or are plagued by demons of doubt or the Enemy Mind attacks or whatever, there will be people around us to help us pull our head out of our ass. Then there's the flipside—someone saying, "Lets go get fucked up and talk about it." You know how many people solve their problems doing that? Zip. Zero. Zilch. Dealing with your issues in that way only magnifies them.

So take inventory constantly. Monitor your friendships and who you spend your time with. See what those relationships and friendships are based on. If it's not to bring about positive change but a destructive end, cut 'em loose. At the beginning of my journey I had to spend a lot of time alone, because quite honestly there weren't too many people back in 1981 on the punk scene in NYC or on the streets getting down with higher knowledge.

Alone time is important to a degree, but we're not by nature loners. We're made for teamwork. It's in our DNA. Why do you think we start this or that society? Because we're part of the human collective. Do you know what society I seek out these days? The PMA society. Those people who can inspire me. Those who thrive even under intense pressure or in adversity. I seek what they have. I beg for their knowledge and wisdom, hoping a bit of what they got will rub off on me. You should do the same.

Start Small, Build Out, Get Your Shit Done

Whenever I'm facing a huge task, to find a place to begin I start by breaking the task down into simple steps. Then I build out to grand leaps and bounds.

Why do this, you ask? Simple. Let's take, for instance, finishing this book. If I just sit there and think, "Holy shit, man, how the hell am I going to write all these pages and fill them with ideas?" The pressure of that question crushes my desire to even begin.

So I start small. I list ideas I'm trying to convey and write them down on index cards. I pin those to the corkboard on my wall. Now I can visualize what has to be done. Visualizing is a vital part of the process. Beginning with breaking a huge task into component parts means I started on it, and that's the main thing—to START. Otherwise, you're just going to be stuck in park, trying to imagine the end of the journey, but you'll never even get your ass in gear.

Remember what I said about value? Good things don't come cheap. It may take weeks, months, even years of preparation to get there, but by learning a few tricks you can keep the mind positively engaged and enjoy the journey. That goes a long way toward finishing something you've started no matter how difficult things get. As long as you're willing to suck it up and push through the inevitable obstacles.

On that note, I want to tell you the story of a girl who went to the same gym a few years back. I observed her for months. When she first came in, she was easily seventy pounds overweight. She decided to give boxing a try. At first you could see she was intimidated. Everyone else was skipping rope like a pro, hitting the bags, and able to do crazy amounts of core and cardio work. Still, she showed up every day with a smile on her face and ground through her workouts. I even saw her puke on one occasion.

Well, I hadn't seen her in awhile because I was traveling, and then when I did, holy shit! I barely recognized her. She had lost all the extra weight and was now one of the people boxing and hitting her reps like a pro. She impressed the shit out of me, and I went up and told her so. She said the reason she was able to do it was because she took it one day at a time and swore never to give up even when she didn't want to train and was sore. The mental tests came, no doubt, but because she set a goal for each day and broke her tasks down, she got through it and achieved her fitness goals.

In Steven Pressfield's amazing book *Do The Work*, he writes, "A child has no trouble believing the unbelievable, nor does the genius or the madman. It's only you and I, with our big brains and our tiny hearts, who doubt and overthink and hesitate."

Personally, I chant the acronym KISS constantly: "Keep It Simple, Stupid." I know not to overcomplicate things by overthinking them. I try to be like that child, believing that anything and everything is possible. You have to keep dreaming. Once you stop, it's a slow death inside.

I know people who gave up on their music, writing, and acting dreams. They even went so far as to tell me I had to "Get real." Well, guess what? They got *real*, all right. They are now *real* miserable, middle-aged fuckers working dead-end jobs, getting drunk at the same shit holes, and talking about their glory years back in the day. As for me, well, I'm just too damn busy living out my dreams to listen to that bullshit.

So do something every day to chip away at your goals. Stay laser focused. Remember, when the demons of doubt arise, it's just your Enemy Mind trying to swerve you off your path. Find the joy and happiness in the positive frame of mind. Love the activity. That way you're not sitting around trying to speculate on what the end result will be. That's not your job. Just start small, build out, do the work, and throw it out into the universe. It's the best mindset to get your shit done!

An exercise:

Want to get in shape? Train for a race? Got a book idea, an idea for a film, an album in you? Trying to figure out your master plan? Maybe start a business? Go get a corkboard, put it up on your wall, and break shit down on index cards. Start small and build out. As the days, weeks, and months go by, you'll see your own progress before your eyes.

Challenge Yourself Daily

Do something that takes you outside your comfort zone. Each day, tackle that thing you've been resisting.

Sign up for that Tough Mudder, make those diet and lifestyle changes, train for your first marathon, a triathlon, join that gym, start that book. Take a step and write a page. Who cares if the outcome sucks in the beginning. Just do it. Ernest Hemingway assured writers that their first draft will be complete shit, yet he kept writing. Resistance hates when you take action. That's why procrastination is its wingman, its drinking buddy.

Again, we come back to the issue of value. You have to be willing to bust your ass. If you always take the coward's way out—"Play it safe, Bob, everything in moderation"—if you're not willing to risk, you'll NEVER get anywhere in life. Welcome the pressure. It builds character.

When I was about to attempt my first Ironman, I'd never even competed in a sprint triathlon before. There were a few of these jock-type a-holes at a bike shop who were like, "I don't know, man. You should do an Olympic distance—even a half Ironman—first. It's crazy to try a full Ironman right out of the box." You know what? Did I listen? Hell, no!

Now, my Ironman coach, Orion Mims, said, "After what this dude's been through in his life, an Ironman's a fucking walk in the park." Well, guess what? I finished. I finished after playing an insane show in Philly the night before, driving straight back to NYC the same night, grabbing a quick shower and stretch, and going to the swim start on NO sleep and with a stress fracture in my foot, I might add. And do I give a fuck that it took me thirteen hours? No. I crossed the line and heard, "John Joseph McGowan, YOU are an Ironman!" That's all that mattered to me on that day. Actually, to be honest, I cried a few tears.

I'm not telling you this to brag, but rather to encourage you to challenge yourself. See what you can accomplish. I'm willing to bet the farm you can do things you've never imagined possible. But only if you take the steps, make the plan, and start—not next week, not tomorrow, but today.

I recently went to hear my good friend Rich Roll speak at a health conference in New York. When he took questions, I asked, "How do we prevent the plateau effect in our training and, more importantly, in our day-to-day life?" In other words, how do we prevent ourselves from coasting and complacency? Rich said, "By constantly doing things that scares us, that challenges us, things we don't know the outcome of but risk doing anyway."

There's that word *risk* again. Sticking to the safe path in life and always staying in your comfort zone stagnates potential. It's a type of creative death of the soul. When you reach outside yourself for more, you develop willpower you never knew you had. In general, we as people never do more than required to get by. That's some part of evolution. We've invented all these machines to minimize the amount work we have to do. In some cases that's a good thing, just not when we're talking about personal growth. Remember this mantra: "Comfort kills productivity."

That's why I must have challenging deadlines and goals. That's what a dream is—an unrealized goal. If I work hard I get there; if I take the easy route I'll never know what I'm truly capable of, what my potential is.

You break out of your comfort zone by doing things differently—in other words, by challenging your set of experiences and values, going against what's been instilled in you and seeking new knowledge. We've each been taught by our parents, teachers, and society a particular way to live, but who says we have to *keep* living that way? Our parents? Their parents? Our teachers? Fuck that. I say question everything and challenge yourself. Everyone who has ever accomplished great things in this world in order to help humanity certainly questioned everything they thought true, and we're all better off because of it. Many people, even some within Dr. Martin Luther King's inner circle, told him he was crazy to march in Selma. Did he listen? No, and because of it the Civil Rights movement took off. By taking great risks and meeting challenges we inspire others to do the same. That's called collective change, and there has never been a time on this planet when collective change is more needed.

People need to test themselves, to push the limits of body and mind. Our nature is to avoid discomfort, to run from what scares us, not toward it. The fact is, you develop a deep sense of self when you push through your fears. Use them as motivation. Pick a fear and challenge it. The other day I heard world-class open water distance swimmer Kim Chambers (who nearly lost her leg) speaking on the Rich Roll podcast. What she said hit home: "The treasure in life lies right on the other side of where you're most fearful." Bingo! Those places are where the real gifts lie in wait, where you hit pay dirt, where you will experience the greatest transformations possible.

When we put ourselves in uncomfortable situations both mentally and physically, it causes brain cells to develop that we never thought we had—new muscles manifest to help us get the job done. We learn more. We grow. And isn't that what life should be about? So don't stagnate. Get out of your comfort zone. Big or small, set challenges and tackle them every single day.

Get-shit-done challenge:

Tackle something today that you have been putting off. Join that gym. Register for that race. Clean the junk food out of the fridge and cupboards. Get that new healthy lifestyle started. No cigarettes or booze for you today, motherfucker. Sure, it's all tough, but successful people willingly place challenge after challenge in front of themselves and conquer them. Again, get out of your comfort zone and go build new physical and mental muscles. As the Marines say, "When the going gets tough, the tough get going."

Have Integrity

Integrity means being honest to one's own values and principles. People with integrity are naturally moral.

Why is integrity important? Simple. You may be able to get over on other people and lie and bullshit your way through life for a while, but eventually you'll be discovered and exposed, landing you in a world of negative shit. When you realize that the only one you can actually cheat is yourself, then you'll do your best to become truthful to yourself and truthful with everyone else.

As far as morals are concerned, you have to stand for something or you'll fall for everything, get hoodwinked, bamboozled. Now, do I give a shit if people don't see eye to eye with me on every single thing? Of course not. Because in my heart of hearts I know what I'm doing is right according to my own moral compass and that's all that matters to me. I stick to my convictions—always have. I've had to develop integrity in my stance on compassion toward animals. When I started to realize I needed to change, everyone criticized me, even laughed. Did I listen? Fuck no. I knew protecting animals was the right thing to do. Matter of fact, I'm even more fired up about this issue today than I was in those days, and I need to be, because the ecology of the planet is a mess and people's health is total shit. Thankfully, though, the science is in and both planet health and people's health can be healed if we switch to an organic, whole foods, plant-based diet. So if you're one of the pseudotough guys who think having compassion is for the weak, you have your head up your ass and are in need of a mental enema. Do yourself a favor—read my last book, *Meat Is for Pussies*.

Bottom line is, you can't please everyone, so don't even try. Just go about your business, stick to your morals, and stay honest in all your dealings.

Treat others the way you want to be treated. Do you want to be bullshitted and lied to? I think not.

I'll tell you this: having integrity in your dealings with others will get you a long way in life. I know many who burned bridges back in the day, who had zero humility, thought they were all that, and would shit on people constantly. These days all they do is bitch and moan on the internet. You need to remember the adage: "Be careful who you treat badly on your way up because you'll be passing them on your way down." *Trinad api sunichena*... Google that. Stay humble, my friends.

Earn Respect

Even back in the day, when I was on the streets and then in lockup, I heard that respect is never given but has to be earned.

I did some stupid, violent shit when I was young just to have the older nutjobs I hung out with on the street respect me. It was time and circumstance, though. New York City was buck wild and I was just a kid alone out there. I had to be tough or I'd become the hunted.

These days, however, I have a different value system. I don't give two craps if some violent, street-urchin, drug-dealing scumbag respects me. But I most certainly do try to earn the respect of people I look up to and admire. The A-type personalities. Their respect doesn't come easy or cheap. Again, that's why it's essential you act with integrity in all your dealings. Many don't agree with my stance on certain things, but I've been told time and again that regardless, they respect my integrity.

So what's the first step in developing integrity? Respect and be honest with yourself. If you don't do that, how can you expect others to respect or be honest with you? Self-respect is something you gain by practicing PMA.

Take action every single day to better yourself and then use respect, humility, and integrity in your dealings with others.

I know some of the most badass dudes on the planet, and they're also the most respectful and humble toward others because they have nothing to prove. The opposite is also true: empty barrels make the most noise. They're also the biggest ego maniac douchebags.

The real test is how you treat others you can't gain something from. When you show an attitude of service and respect through your actions and not just your words, and you practice that day after day, you become a more positive person. It changes your moral compass and makes you someone people look up to and respect. Not that you should do anything simply to be glorified, but we have to set an example. We must have enough courage to go out on a limb and stick to our convictions no matter what the circumstances or what others might think.

Let's imagine again how successful a society we could be if everyone practiced respect for themselves and others, if they all remained humble. If instead of judging and criticizing we showed love and respect, just imagine what could happen? Again, I'm not someone that throws the word *love* into every other sentence, but I'm also man enough to say that it's what the world needs more of in these crazy times. Respecting others is the first step in loving them.

If we're truly trying to better ourselves and this planet, that endeavor comes with a hefty price, but it's one worth paying. Respect encourages kindness, demands integrity, honor, and acknowledgement of the value of another living creature on the planet, whether great or small. If you want to change the destructive course humankind is on, develop and maintain this mood.

Set Goals and Visualize

As of late I've been doing some motivational speaking at inner-city schools and even to young adults in prisons. Many of these kids are in gangs, come from broken families, and are using drugs. The ones who are locked up have made mistakes, but there's still hope for them. I can relate; I've been there.

One of the first schools I spoke at was out in Bed-Stuy, Brooklyn. When I walked in I heard one of the kids say, "Who is this white motherfucker trying to tell me some shit?" Well, as we sat in that library and I told my story, their attitudes changed. They could see past my skin color to the fact that I was indeed one of them.

The next thing I did was pull out my passport to show them that I've been all over the world in my travels as a musician, author,

Ironman, and speaker. Then I asked, "Do you know where 99 percent of all the dudes I ran the streets with or was locked up with back in the day have gone? Back to jail, an early grave, or back to the streets, homeless and drug-addicted." The point I wanted them to get is that you have to set goals. You can't float aimlessly through life. I asked them what they wanted to do with their lives. Many didn't know.

I tell them they have to dream outside the box. They have to visualize what it is they want to do in life and then go for it. Be all in.

We need to have goals, and when we find that "thing"—it's back to the corkboard. Write it down and pin it up. Then you can take the necessary actions to achieve it.

You make a roadmap toward a goal. And that's when the next phase comes—routine discipline. When you set a goal, you go after it. You allocate time for it, you beat the Enemy Mind with a stick every day and make it happen. You don't make excuses. That's why I have zero time for bullshit. It's all about challenging myself by constantly establishing goals, eliminating obstacles to the best of my ability, and keeping routine discipline.

The military knows all about routine discipline. In training they make you do things over and over just to make sure you get it right, that you're paying attention to detail. In yoga practice routine disciple is *sadhana*. Having a routine and working hard at it is a sure way to strive for perfection. If I know I have to finish my next book, film, or race, you best believe that shit's up on my corkboard so I can visualize my goal and take the routine disciplined steps to smash the fuck out of it. Every time you finish something you start, you develop confidence and a can-do, positive attitude.

Robert McKee always tells his students that he makes no guarantees about what will happen if they finished their screenplays, but he did promise us what will happen if we don't: nothing. Again, it comes down to having a passion for something and doing it because you love it, regardless of the result. In the beginning you get credit just for showing up. But then you have to stay motivated mentally and physically, continue to set the bar high, stay challenged, and stay the course. As Rich Roll says, set goals that scare you and do your best to smash them.

When you're setting goals, make both short-and long-term ones. The short-term ones give you small victories that build self-confidence and help you push on to the long-term ones. I find that the happiest, most successful people are those who constantly set and accomplish goals. But be realistic. Setting goals you can't yet achieve—for instance, planning to run a marathon you know you don't have time to train for—gets you nowhere, because when you don't get the desired result, you'll feel negative, and a quitter's mentality will kick in. That can be a road to depression. So be realistic with your goalsetting in the beginning. Yes, I signed up for an Ironman right out of the box, but I also knew I'd get it done because I had the work ethic to do it. I trained my ass off with my coach, which meant that achieving the goal became more realistic. My expectations of success were matched by my desire and willingness and preparation to get it done.

So set incremental goals that can lead toward your larger objective. Achieving these will build self-confidence and reinforce your positive mindset. I'm not saying you can't finish an Ironman or a marathon, but if you try it right out the box without training, you're usually setting yourself up for failure. As I said earlier, start small and build out. That's what I do with everything. The first step is visualization. I'm telling you right now, if you follow suit, nothing can stand in the way of achieving your goals.

Try this:

Take a moment each day to stop the flood of superfluous bullshit rushing through your head. Turn off all exterior forms of communication—your cell phone, computer, TV, radio. Look inward and focus. Create a visual image of the work you're going to do and the steps you'll take to achieve it. Visualization is important. When I prepare for a race, I see myself in the water, in transition, on the bike, tackling the run. It works. Setting goals, visualizing the process, then taking the necessary steps leads to success. If you can dream it, you can be it.

Look for a Mentor

One who thinks he or she has it all figured out is fool #1. All of us can benefit from a mentor—someone who can watch us, offer insights, guide us in an area of our lives, whether that's our career, our spiritual path, our sobriety. That's why people in twelve-step programs get sponsors.

Let's use the example of kids on a sports team. There's a coach, right? Well, the coach is a mentor. Unfortunately, when we grow up we think we no longer need a mentor. That's a huge mistake. Oprah says, "A mentor is someone who allows you to see the hope inside yourself." Everything about PMA, about success, about achieving your goals, is based on a willingness to learn continuously. For that we need mentors. Don't be that old dog—the one who can't be taught new tricks.

We always shoot for the stars, aim high, focus on what we want to achieve. But how will we succeed if we never share our plans with a mentor who has walked the path before us.

Someone who can look at our plans from a different perspective is helpful. When a pilot's flying in zero visibility in bad weather, he has to rely on radar and the air traffic controller. Similarly, accepting instructions from a mentor helps get you to your destination.

You also become more committed when others are invested in seeing you reach your dreams. The key to any relationship with a mentor, teacher, guru, or sensei is to be diligent about choosing a good one. There are many charlatans out there, and if you mistakenly choose one of these parasites, you're screwed, at least for a while. There are those who teach simply to bolster their egos. They want to lord it over and control their mentees, not help them. If I know there's a thief in the room and I don't warn you to safeguard your valuables, how am I your friend? So that's what I'm doing here. Heed the advice. Choose wisely and, when you do find the right mentor, surrender to the teacher-student relationship.

Each One Teach One

If you get a gift, pay it forward. That's how the deal works. Knowledge is the greatest gift I've received. What brings me the greatest happiness is to pass that knowledge on.

Nothing will put you in a better mindset than to reach out to those who need your help.

> **Honestly, I have to say helping others is at the top of my daily to-do list in my PMA practice. Taking time to help others is noble.**

I'd never be where I am today if others hadn't helped me. I can never forget my duty to repay that. Life is a test, my friends—a test to see what kind of character we really have—what we do and how we treat people when the cameras are off and there's no praise.

There's a term in bhakti yoga that says, "True devotional service must be unmotivated and uninterrupted."

Kahlil Gibran, author of *The Prophet,* writes, "There are those who give with joy, and that joy is their reward." In other words, act selflessly, not expecting payback for your service. When you do this you take the focus off yourself and your ego and look to the greater human collective. It's not about what have you done for me lately but rather what I've done for them. When society loses touch with this ancient wisdom we become focused on "I, me, mine." Imagine millions of people with this selfish attitude and we'll have today's world.

Remember, actions speak volumes over words. Be a person of action, not someone offering lip service. Be a role model who knows example is better than precept.

If we lead by example, if we *do,* people will follow. Anytime I tell my friends I'm cooking and going out to feed the homeless, and I invite friends to help, they line up. Good leaders lead from the front. I believe that those of you who are now taking the time to read this book truly do have a desire to improve yourself and the planet. Why shouldn't you try to mentor others, to pay it forward? With humility, of course. If you have achieved positive results, people *should* follow your lead.

That's not ego talking; it's the process of positive collective change at work, and God knows we need it in these crazy-ass times we're living in, especially the American youth. I've personally witnessed kids and adults do amazing 180s because somebody gave a fuck enough to reach out and mentor them, to give them guidance and advice. Those mentors took time out of their busy day and gave a shit. Giving a shit is Compassion 101.

I know of no better way to become a better human being—and to gain and maintain PMA—than to mentor and help others. I try and remind myself of this every day. I even began signing my emails and letters "Your friend in service, John Joseph" just to drive the point home and remember that my purpose in this life is SERVICE.

Others before me have sacrificed much by serving others in order to make the world a better place. My guru, Srila Prabhupada, left India at seventy years old, boarded a steamship with seven dollars and a case of his books, crossed two oceans in treacherous conditions, and arrived in New York City alone! Even had two heart attacks on the way. He landed on the Lower East Side and taught bhakti yoga for free, slept on the floor, lived with no possessions, and went out daily to chant in public. One of the first things he did when he had a handful of followers is print Vedic knowledge and distribute it and feed the needy. In his mind, everyone was needy—his food was an offering of love, and he could think of no one who didn't need love. Imagine that level of selflessness and dedication to mentoring others.

Some have given their lives to helping others. They've believed strongly in helping others as a way to make the world a better place. They know it only takes one person at a time to change, and that individual change leads to changing everything. If we truly believe in what we're doing, we'll risk everything, including our lives, to do it. As Dr. King said, "Life's most persistent and urgent question is, what are you doing for others?"

There's always more of ourselves to give. On my path it's stated that Krishna (God) wants from us what we're holding back. Krishna wants us to give it to others in order to help them on their path. We don't lose when we give; we gain. The path of bhakti yoga is based on serving others. In the big scheme of things, it's not just about personal growth but the growth of everyone. We have to become team players. As the saying goes, we're only as strong as our weakest link. Empowering others by mentoring them is the most effective thing you can do to make a difference in the world.

Health Is Wealth—
Stop Eating that Crap

"When the diet is wrong, medicine is of no use; when the diet is correct, there is no need for medicine."

—*Ayurvedic proverb*

Come on now, you knew this shit was coming from a dude whose last book was called *Meat is For Pussies.*

But it isn't just the meat that fucks you up. As that book states, it's all the other bad shit as well—the processed food, the dairy, the GMOs, preservatives, and chemically treated foods, the smokes, the booze, and the laziness. So let's get this out of the way right now. If you don't make the necessary changes to what you're ingesting every day, you'll never get anywhere in this process. It's like trying to light a fire and throwing water on it at the same time.

I can speak from personal experience on this because the catalyst for my change came when I gave a thought to what the hell I was eating. That was the spark that lit the fire. When I cared about the vehicle housing me, the passenger-soul, when I stopped all the bad shit—crap food, drugs, alcohol—then the light came on.

I can't stress enough how important proper food choices are. They affect your emotions and thoughts, they change your body right down on the cellular level, and they affect your consciousness.

People tend to forget this mind-body-soul connection when it comes to food. You see, when you wake up and decide to eat healthy, it means you give a shit. Your body will thank you for it. Your frame of mind and your consciousness become positive. You'll then look for ways to improve other areas of your life.

The opposite reaction is there if you don't eat properly. If you sit around checking your Facebook all day, gossiping, playing hours' worth of video games, spending your nights in the bars and fast-food shit shacks, your body will break down. It'll get diseased. You'll also be in a bad mood most of the time and more than likely will be spiraling downward into a serious case of depression.

Think of your body as if it were your car. You are the soul, the driver, within. You witness everything. Now, if you want this vehicle to carry you through your life properly, just like with your car you have to do the maintenance. You have to put the right stuff in. Unfortunately, these days people seem to care more about the upkeep of their cars than they do about their bodies. That shit has to stop, because trust me, an unmaintained vehicle can only be speeding toward a very nasty head-on collision.

But, if my words aren't enough, do yourself a favor and go visit a kidney dialysis center, cancer ward, or hospital where people are fighting for their lives. Ask them if they wish they'd taken better care of their bodies, or if they'd do things differently had they realized the consequences of their actions.

These days, quite a number of people are starting to wake up, leaving their dinosaur diets behind—you know, the meat and potatoes, artery-clogging, cheesy, gastrointestinal nightmare bullshit they were forcefed as children and taught to think was good for them. In part, the wake-up is because they're sick and tired of being sick and tired. Their quality of life is shit, and they're shelling out hundreds a month for meds to treat curable diseases like IBS, Crohn's disease, high blood pressure, heart disease, Type 2 diabetes, high cholesterol, and the rest—all of which are related to diet and lifestyle.

It's fucking insane how many Americans are on meds these days. There is a health crisis in this country, an obesity epidemic. True of other developed countries around the world too. And it's because of what we are stuffing into our faces. The tide *is* beginning to turn on this now, though, because people who've switched to a whole foods, plant-based, non-GMO, organic diet have been able to say goodbye to their bottles of pills. Some of them were even near death. But they've reversed their health issues.

Now, you and I love to hear stories like that. They inspire us, motivate us to change. Do you know who hates them, though, and who is in fact losing sleep over it? The pharmaceutical company execs. To counteract the positive wave that's starting they've embarked on a campaign of bullshit lies and false information, even paying off their goons in the FDA and USDA to go after the true healers.

The American Heart Association, American Diabetes Association, American Cancer Society, as well as research companies *supposedly* looking for a cure for cancer, like the Susan G. Komen Foundation and their pink-ribbon bullshit are actually taking big money, along with the others—billions in fact—from these same companies who are putting out the products that are causing the disease. Go on their websites. They actually encourage you to eat those poisonous foods as part of a healthy diet. That is some straight-up scumbag shit of the lowest form, and the government is in bed with all those parasites. Want proof? Just watch the amazing, ground-breaking 2017 documentary, *What the Health*. The money is not in the cure, it's in the pills for the symptoms and the endless fundraising for research. Those people are lining their pockets with cash.

The other reason many men in the fitness world (women have been up on it) who are trying to turn the corner on bad health have switched to a plant-based diet is because they've seen the amount of beasts out there like Rich Roll, Rip Esselstyn, Brendan Brazier, UFC fighter Mac Danzig, The NFL's "300-lb Vegan" David Carter, bodybuilder Robert Cheeke, and on and on. None of these dudes are passing out from lack of nutrients. There is no "protein deficiency." As a matter of fact, they're at the top of their game. So if you need a mentor to change your health, follow their lead. They know what's up.

FACT: You can't outtrain a bad diet. That's why I eat meals loaded with high-level, organic, plant-based nutrients. The body is a machine. Regulate it, do the necessary maintenance, work out, eat right every day, and that machine will run like a badass. I see so many people training hard in the gym but then making shit food choices.

I've been at this for over thirty-seven years and I'm dialed in on my nutrition. It's helped me keep a positive mindset even in some of my darkest hours. A healthy body is a healthy mind. When people wake up and eat crap like bacon, eggs, and greasy fried potatoes, toast, butter, and coffee and the rest, it's like throwing a wrench in the works. And if that's not bad enough, when your body has to work so hard to digest all that poison, the mental processes slow too. You go into a food coma. You've seen it. People passing out on the train in the morning, drooling on the person next to them. Definitely don't make bad food choices at night either—all of that crap rotting in your colon, boiling like toxic sludge, will cause acid reflux.

Eat to live; don't live to eat. Food is fuel. Food gives me crazy energy to thrive in my training, which I know I must do in order to remain balanced. People always ask what a typical day of eating looks like for me. So here you go.

FIVE DAILY BULLET POINTS FOR HEALTH

1. **Always drink clean water when you wake up in order to flush the body of toxins.** You can even put a little organic apple cider vinegar in it to help remove toxic waste in the body. I try to drink at least a gallon of water a day every day. I even bought a water filtration system because I hate the fluoride and other chemicals in city water, and buying water in plastic bottles is bad for you and the environment. So make the investment. Get the poisons out of your water. You'll save a lot of money in the end, and by the way, cook with that clean water as well.

2. **Never skip breakfast, and always eat as little processed food as possible at that meal.** Fresh juices, fruits, sprouted whole grains—I like to eat as much raw food as possible in the morning because raw foods are alive with enzymes and don't slow my digestive system down. Also, if you fail to prepare, prepare to fail, so bring good food to work. Otherwise you might get tempted to make that hellish fast-food shit-shack stop with your coworkers. No bueno!

3. **Complex carbohydrates are fuel. Don't skip on them and follow those crazy "no-carb," "low-carb" diets or that whack-ass Paleo diet.** Those dudes are headed for a heart attack, trust me. The Paleo

diet bullshit is nothing more than a rebranding of that Atkins diet crap. Just avoid bad carbs like processed flour and grains loaded with oil.

4. **Eliminate ALL animal proteins. You don't need them. They're highly acidic and stress the body. Always remember that meat is from rotting corpses.** There are dozens of plant-based protein options out there. Use Google. Remember, knowledge is power. Learn, study, read, educate yourself. Watch *Forks over Knives, Food Choices, Eating you Alive, What the Health, Simply Raw, Vegucated*. There are others. All of them present the truth about food. These films are real game changers, which is, by the way, the title of another movie that will be out in 2018.

5. **Eat a wide variety of foods and learn how to cook them. I did, and its why I've been able to stick to my path.** I learned more about food as I learned to cook it. It's amazing how far the plant-based diet has come in restaurants over the last few decades. That's why I crack up when people ask, "What do you eat, salads?" I'm like, "What the fuck do *you* eat, KFC, Mickey Dee's, and Jack-off in the Box?" Look, don't stay stuck on stupid, like these 1980s, Momma-luke throwbacks in their tiger-striped workout pants, walking around drinking from three-gallon jugs of God-knows-what and asking me where I get my protein. Do some damn research and find out why the plant power movement is catching on.

If you're transitioning from the Standard American Diet (SAD, and yes, it's sad) and need meat substitutes, go for it. Just make sure they're non-GMO and organic. Take your time. Don't stress or obsess. Stay chill. We don't need any more macropsychotics running around out there. Stress causes disease and can cancel the benefits of a healthy lifestyle. I want you to make progress and gain ground you won't retreat from in the war against disease.

Food for thought: What we choose to eat is responsible for much more than our own health. Environmentally, meat, dairy, fish, eggs—all animal production—is destroying the planet. Don't believe the hype the corporations pushing this crap have thrown out to you over the years, attaching negative stereotypes to environmentalists as if saving the planet is something dumb. I mean, are these people fucking stupid or what? We live here. We destroy it. Where the fuck are we supposed to go, Pluto? That's just ignorance. If you have kids, you need to think about what you're leaving them, and what about their kids and future generations? How can you refuse to change? Watch the amazing documentary *Cowspiracy* to see the real environmental impact your food choices have on the earth.

I also need to mention the badass karma involved in confining, torturing, killing, and eating all these animals. If you truly want to attain PMA, you have to think about all aspects of life on planet earth, not just the ones we think are important. How many people clean Fido's ass with baby wipes and then let him sleep in their beds, licking his balls on your pillow while you support the animal industry's death camps. We can't bury our heads in the sand anymore. We have to turn the corner on this now and decide that what we put in our shopping carts and on our dinner tables is a HUGE step toward saving the planet and ultimately ourselves. If you want help on understanding this, pick up a copy of my book *Meat is For Pussies*. I've given great info and tons of easy to make recipes all up in that bad boy. PMA and plants for the win!

Exercise Like You Give a Fuck

The *New York Times* recently wrote an article on a new study published in *JAMA Internal Medicine* that helps shed light on how important regular exercise is:

"Researchers with the National Cancer Institute, Harvard University, and other institutions gathered and pooled data about people's exercise habits from six large, ongoing health surveys, winding up with information about more than 661,000 adults, most of them middle-aged.

"Using this data, the researchers stratified the adults by their weekly exercise time, from those who did not exercise at all to those who worked out for ten times the current recommendations or more [meaning that they exercised moderately for twenty-five hours or more per week.] Then they compared fourteen years' worth of death records for the group. They found that, unsurprisingly, the people who did not exercise at all were at the highest risk of early death. But those who exercised a little, not meeting the recommendations but doing something, lowered their risk of premature death by 20 percent."

Got it?

Even a *little* exercise every day can improve your health and help you live longer. Studies also show that people who exercise regularly benefit by a positive mood boost and lower rates of depression.

When you exercise, your body releases chemicals called endorphins. Endorphins trigger a positive feeling in the body and mind not so different from what morphine does. For example, the feeling that follows a run or workout is often described as euphoric. That feeling, known as a "runner's high," is usually accompanied by a positive and energizing outlook on life.

There's just no excuse for sitting on your ass and being lazy. Don't bitch and moan about how your life sucks if you don't take the initiative to change it. Reduce your nonsense activities, like watching hours of TV, playing video games, or trolling the internet, and replace them with exercise. I'm not telling you to go out and run marathons or do an Ironman, but even some brisk walking will turn the tables on your mood and health. Remember, every journey starts with that first step, so get to steppin'.

Many people who work out keep a training log, but you should also keep a nutrition log. You can't outtrain a bad diet, so monitor not only what you eat but when you eat it and how it made you feel. In other words, do you eat when you're stressed or down in the dumps? Often, people eat to self-medicate when they're feeling down. They feel great for a few minutes during and after eating their so-called delicious treats from hell, but then they feel guilty or drained of energy, so they have reduced productivity. I'm speaking from experience. I've self-medicated with food too and paid the price.

The U.S. and most of the developed world is in poor health and overweight, and this leads to debilitating disease, depression, and ultimately the vicious cycle of prescriptions meds. That only furthers the downward spiral. I attribute a lot of the way we eat to corporations hiding their dirty little lies in food commercials, which make their crap look so enticing. Don't fall for it. Watch the films I mentioned. They paint the real picture of what's going down.

The paradigm is beginning to shift, though, as people look for a way out. Just yesterday I got an email from a bona fide tough guy, who admitted he had been skeptical about plant-based eating, meditation, and the whole PMA lifestyle. He also admitted he was unhealthy, depressed, and riddled with anxiety, which he curbed by drinking and taking recreational drugs along with his prescribed antidepressants.

His shift came when he started dating a chick who was a healthy herbivore. She urged him to give it a try, and he did. Well, just like so many others before him, his mood, health, and life changed for the better. He's off all the drugs, he's alcohol-free, works out, and has lost a shitload of weight. He said his only regret was that he waited so long to make the change. See that? PMA is contagious.

I've noticed that most grumpy people don't exercise. Shit, I'm guilty of some male PMS my damn self when I don't get to exercise. But as soon as them beads of sweat begin to drip, my mood improves. Studies also prove that a healthy diet and regular exercise reduce stress, ward off anxiety and depression, boost self-esteem, and improve sleep. So have a green juice, get off your ass, and stop bitching. Beat the blues with a jog, a trip to the gym, a bike ride, or get in the pool. Revolution can begin in the muscles. Just make sure you let that revolution be complete by having proper nutrition.

I've ended this first section with diet and exercise because I know the value of both in attaining a positive mindset, or PMA. After releasing *Meat Is for Pussies* and doing a bunch of video shoots for Vice, Munchies, and other outlets, thousands of people have followed suit, become vegans, and written to tell me of their amazing transformations. I answer every damn email or message I receive because it makes me so happy to know that others are on the path and have improved their lives or perhaps even cheated death. All it takes is applying knowledge and some determination. So I challenge you to take what you've read so far and apply it. When you do that, I'll be answering your emails and messages too.

PART TWO

Let's Dig Deep

Here we break down the workings of the mind and what separates those who accomplish their goals from those who don't. I'll also give you some tools to help you sharpen your mental skills.

The Nature of the Mind: Thinking-Feeling-Willing

The mind is a very tricky, cagey fucker. As I said, unless it's controlled and then properly engaged, it can become your worst enemy.

Sit back and think about that statement for a minute, because it's deep. Is your worst enemy ever going to tell you to do something that's advantageous for your happiness and success? I think not. It'll be more like, "Yo, John, go 'head, smoke that crack and fuck everyone over. You only live once, homeboy, so go for yours." That's no bullshit, so allow me to elaborate.

In 1988, because of a series of events that went bad in my life, I was out on the streets again, living in burned-out buildings in Alphabet City and strong-arm robbing some very dangerous people. Basically, I was a lowlife crackhead. But I wasn't your typical crackhead. Hell, no. I worked out and became very efficient with all types of weapons. I also had a violent streak you definitely did *not* want to meet on a dark street, especially if I needed to get high. I'm not boasting—just telling it like it is.

I was involved in a number of life-and-death scenarios because of drugs, including a Colombian coke dealer who, when I was jonesing, made the mistake of getting into my car to sell me a few ounces of coke I had no intention of paying for. The robbery went south when it turned out he had a .45 and tried to shoot me.

There were also KOS ("kill-on-sight") orders put out on me by crack dealers, because I'd done so many strong-armed robberies. One of those near-death experiences—this time, in Miami, when a dude I was freebasing with failed to mention that the pound of coke he had was stolen from some crazy Cuban Cocaine Cowboys. Well, the dude splits and says it's cool to stay at his house (thanks, motherfucker), and at 5 a.m. two days later they show up with AR-15s and fire over thirty rounds into the room where I was sleeping before spraying the rest of the house.

Just a few of the situations I've been in, thanks to my Enemy Mind. As I said, I shouldn't be alive. The fact that I am means I no longer take a single day for granted or lose sight of the fact that a few people reached out when everyone else turned their back on me or kept their distance because I was so damn volatile and unpredictable.

My problems stemmed from the fact that as major obstacles arose in my life, they opened old wounds—cutting at scar tissue left from a very abusive childhood. I'd tried to bury all that shit in my subconscious. I mean, consider what it does to a kid's mind to find out that the people he thought took him into their home to love him only did it for money. Their real kids lived like kings while we were abused, neglected, starved. It recently occurred to me that for the entire seven years we were in that foster home, those people never took a single photograph of us. We were ghost children, our entire childhoods stolen. I went through life pretending like those things didn't matter, didn't get to me, but they did. They were lying in wait. Then, as life's pressures increased and I was tested, I failed miserably and resorted to addiction and violence just to cope.

These days, I sit back and monitor my thoughts. I've learned not to identify with them but instead to be separate or aloof from them.

I'm not my mind. If something negative arises, I know I have to shift my mind from those thoughts and attach it to something positive. That's the intelligence kicking in when you do that. The intelligence is above the mind and five senses. We should let our intelligence direct us: "Hey, you know what'll happen if you do that shit, right?"

That's why I call bullshit on all this new-age crap about emptying the mind of all thoughts. The real deal? It can't be done. As Arjuna tells Krishna in the Bhagavad Gita while the two of them are standing on the Battlefield of Kurukshetra surrounded by armies,

> **"For the mind is restless, turbulent, obstinate, and very strong, O Krishna, and to subdue it is, it seems to me, more difficult than controlling the wind."**

What did Krishna tell Arjuna to do about that? Engage the mind in the higher self. In other words, bring the mind under control by constant meditation on your Higher Power. Only then will there remain nothing left to agitate the mind. I think the fact this was spoken to Arjuna, a warrior facing death, is significant. Inevitably, we too are facing death. We too battle our Enemy Mind. Take a page from the Gita and do what Arjuna did—he fought. We too must fight to fix the mind on the higher self with the help of the intelligence. Practice this and live it daily.

An Uncontrolled Mind Can Lead Us Right to Addiction

One thing I've learned first-hand from the circles in which I was raised is that trying to ignore traumas and push them into the subconscious is a recipe for disaster.

The Enemy Mind never forgets them. It knows exactly when to call its soldiers forth, and at the point when you're most vulnerable, for those soldiers to sink their daggers into your psyche.

So always get things off your chest. Talk them out with someone you love and trust or, if you need it, get guidance from a professional. Never keep trauma bottled up. Don't bury pain, because as life's pressures mount, I can guarantee you with 100 percent certainty that your trauma will rear its ugly head.

It's the nature of the mind to think about something, then feel about it, and then will it to happen. Maybe you're having a stretch of tough times. At every turn things go south—career, relationships, friends. You're questioning everything; you're paralyzed. At that point, some negative idea will manifest on the subtle level—that is, you'll think about it, even meditate on it. Next you'll feel attracted or repulsed or both by it, like you want to do it but you don't want to do it. All emotion, you let the urge kick in. Then before you know it, you end up like me, smoking crack, sipping gin and juice, risking life and limb to get high, and justifying everything you do because you had a rough childhood.

So take inventory. See yourself as apart from your mind and recognize those negative thoughts when they appear. Then use that which is above the mind—the intelligence—to understand the consequences of the action you're contemplating. Intelligence, as I mentioned, has three levels. Be first-class intelligent. Be that person who can hear some wisdom and do the right thing.

You can use your mind to accomplish amazing things—to get where you want to be, for example. As long as you can differentiate between the real you and the subtle parts of your conditioned self—your mind, intelligence, and false ego. Don't let these terms confuse you. It's actually very simple. You say "My mind, my intelligence, my ego," right? Well, who is that *you*? Who *are* you? You're not the body, mind, senses, or intelligence. Who are you who possesses those faculties? Sit back, be mindful, and give that some thought.

Doing these mental and intellectual exercises is an important part of the PMA process. Why? Because doing them let's you deal with the self and not just your mind. Plus they're a way to constantly engage the mind, to keep it occupied. We all know that an idle mind is the devil's workshop, and in that workshop you'll find fear, doubt, depression, and defeat. Those four never start out full-blown; they creep up on you, grab hold of you little by little, and never let go. I've seen many go down that path and let the Enemy Mind conquer them. Then they're consumed by doubt and fear, which makes them quit their goals and dreams. Once that happens, depression can set in, and it shows up with its crew: drugs and alcohol. It's a downward spiral from there, and it all began because instead of taking a positive action to combat negative thoughts these persons froze and did nothing. They couldn't do anything because they didn't know who they were. So they were lost to the enemy.

Always remember, we're talking about what you can accomplish with a positive *mental* attitude. You can only do that if you learn to bridle the mind.

If you're on a chariot drawn by wild, out-of-control horses, it can get downright ugly for you, and who knows where you'll end up? The mind can crush you—and it will. It's happened to me, so I'm telling you from my own experience. It searches for the smallest crack in your armor. "Ah, Johnny boy, fuck doing your workout today and fuck writing. There's always tomorrow." The Enemy Mind is full of shit, so don't listen to it. Instead, make it work for you. Bridle that horse and get it to plow the fields of resistance, planting seeds of determination and hard work. Then let it help you harvest the fruits of your labor.

On that note I'll leave you with a great example of what I'm getting at from the timeless classic, *Bhagavad Gita As It Is,* by A. C. Bhaktivedanta Swami Prabhupada: "The chariot stands for the human body. The five horses which draw the chariot are the five sense organs. The reins stand for the mind, and the charioteer stands for the intellect. The rider here is the individual *jiva* [you, the soul]. If the charioteer falls asleep or is not alert, then the reins which are to be controlled by the charioteer will become loose and then the horses will go out of control. This then ends up in the destruction of the chariot and the rider." (Text 6.34, purport)

An Iron Will Manifests Through Discipline

"Discipline is the bridge between goals and accomplishment."

—Jim Rohn

One of the many things I love about having been on this journey over the last thirty-five years is the number of amazing people I've had the pleasure and good fortune to meet, especially those who've had phenomenal achievements while inspiring countless others to do the same.

I've even had the privilege of becoming good friends with many of them. One such person is my good friend Rich Roll. Rich's story is worth mentioning here, since he was voted one of the world's twenty-five fittest dudes in *Men's Health,* his podcast is in the top ten on iTunes, and his memoir, *Finding Ultra,* is a #1 bestseller.

Rich has been a top finisher at the 2008 and 2009 Ultraman World Championships in Hawaii, considered by many to be one of the world's most grueling endurance races. Ultraman is a three-day, 320-mile double Ironman distance triathlon that circumnavigates the entire Big Island. Day 1 involves a 6.2 mile ocean swim, followed immediately by a ninety-mile crosscountry bicycle race. Day 2 is a 170-mile cycling race. The event culminates on Day 3 with a fifty-two-mile double marathon run on the searing hot lava fields of the Kona coast.

In 2009, Rich returned to Ultraman twice and, despite a stacked field, took home first-day honors with a blistering 2:21 swim victory (sixth fastest of all time) and a third fastest bike leg, to win the day with a ten-minute lead. On Day 2 Rich suffered a serious bike crash, but he managed to salvage the day by winning sixth place overall. Despite his injured knee and shoulder, Rich nonetheless went on to a 7:51 Day 3 double-marathon, holding onto sixth place overall. In May 2010, Rich and his Ultra colleague Jason Lester accomplished an unprecedented feat of staggering endurance many thought impossible—something they call the Epic 5—five Ironman distance triathlons on five islands of Hawaii in under a week.

I have to say that even with all of his astonishing accomplishments, Rich is one of the humblest, most spiritually grounded, genuine dudes I know on the planet. What makes his story truly *epic* is what he had to overcome to be the badass dude he is today. You see, it wasn't always about fitness for Rich. After graduating from Stanford University (where he was a competitive swimmer) and then Cornell law school, he struggled with drugs and alcohol—addictions that fucked up his life for a decade, landing him in jails, institutions, and rehab at age 31. Although he finally did get sober, Rich found himself fifty pounds overweight and the farthest thing from fit. He was eating what he called the "window" diet: if he could pull up to a drive-in window and order it, he ate it. Everything came to a head for him on his fortieth birthday when he walked up a flight of stairs and doubled over in pain. He'd had a close call with a heart attack. That was his "inciting incident," his crisis. He knew he needed to make some major changes and quick.

The day after his staircase epiphany, Rich overhauled his diet, became a dedicated vegan, put on his running shoes, and jumped back into the pool. It wasn't long before ambition took hold and his quest to participate in Ultraman slowly developed. Two years later and fifty pounds lighter—and fueled by nothing but plants—Rich surprised the triathlon & Ultra communities by being not only the first vegan to complete the 320-mile über endurance event but by finishing among the top ten males and becoming the third fastest American. He had the second fastest swim split—all without ever having completed in even a half-Ironman distance triathlon. But what's really crazy is less than two years before his first Ultraman, Rich didn't even own a bike.

Consider the mental toughness, focus, and *discipline* Rich required to do what he did. Every day, beating down his mind with a stick, choosing to accomplish his tasks, and so beating addiction, bad diet, and weight issues all while taking on the world's toughest endurance challenges. I mean, shit, I'm just an average Ironman and know what it is to just finish one of those things, but five in seven days?

Guys like Rich know you can't be successful in anything substantial in life without willpower, and that willpower only manifests through routine discipline. I don't give a shit how smart you are; you have to stay focused and disciplined to get anywhere in this world. You have to have a plan and then execute it. If you float through life without a plan, it's only natural that you'll find yourself surrendering and caving to the dictates of your enemy mind and thus setting yourself up for a life of misery. That's why I keep writing down my plans and putting them on my corkboard. Then I execute again and again.

Well-disciplined people are also perseverant. They have self-control and are not easily allured by distractions that draw them away from what they're trying to achieve.

Discipline creates self-confidence and self-esteem. Even when there are mini setbacks and failures, well-disciplined persons push on. They have clear goals. They get up early each morning prepared to fight like hell to remove obstacles on their paths. Discipline allows them to sacrifice instant, cheap gratification for meaningful, long-term goals.

Lack of discipline, however, works in the opposite way. It creates doubt, failure, health and relationship problems, addiction, laziness, procrastination, and impulsive acting out. I can't begin to tell you how many times I've seen people, including myself, get caught up in a world of shit. If I analyze why we were in that position, all I have to do is look at how we each lacked discipline.

Discipline is dependent on courage. It takes courage to step out into the unknown and try something new, to admit, "Hey, bro, maybe I'm doing things the wrong way." Shit, admitting this was the first step in my process. So find the courage to face the pain and difficulty in doing those new tasks. Establish fresh goals continuously and then follow through on executing them. As you begin to accumulate small victories, your self confidence will grow and discipline will come more naturally.

Yesterday, I overheard someone say that a fool with a plan is better than a genius without one. That's so true. I know some very smart people who never amounted to shit because they lacked discipline—they had no plan, so there was nothing to work toward. Worse, they had dozens of plans, but never executed any of them, never saw even one through to the end. Don't be that guy or girl. Use the formula. Have a plan. Write it down. Execute. Stay disciplined. Develop willpower and smash your goals.

Vince Lombardi once said, "Mental toughness is many things and rather difficult to explain. Its qualities are sacrifice and self-denial. Also, most importantly, it is combined with a perfectly disciplined will that refuses to give in. It's a state of mind—you could call it character in action."

Five Tips for Developing Discipline

1. Set goals and know what they'll achieve.
2. Have a clear strategy.
3. Identify possible obstacles.
4. Always remain willing to change behaviors (learn new ways).
5. Stay focused.

Seize Opportunities

Opportunity knocks, but it's never been known to kick the damn door down. That's your job.

You have to stay disciplined and go after your goals with unrelenting determination—drive your ambition. Don't be the lazy fool who laments because a golden opportunity slipped through his hands. You're not allowed to be a slacker and then complain when things don't turn out the way you want.

You'll never see determined people do that crap. They know that by staying motivated and showing up they'll get where they need to go in life—maybe not today or tomorrow, but they'll get there eventually. That mindset creates an aura of self-confidence and positive energy. When you feel that, you can't wait for your feet to touch the floor in the morning. You never roll over, hit the snooze button, scratch your ass, fart, and go back to sleep.

Every night before going to bed, I list the goals I need to accomplish the next day and pin them up on my corkboard. There's a method to my madness. If I have a visual on what I need to do, for me, it's manifested. If you have an idea, it doesn't exist until it's written down on that index card, that page in your notebook, that napkin at the dinner table.

Stuck in a rut and want to change? Then recognize openings in a moment where something or someone inspires you. Do something, do *anything,* to improve your life. There are talkers and doers. Define what you want and make the decision to go after it. Be a doer. A lioness spends days stalking her next meal. She has to or her cubs will die. Imagine what you could do if you approached every goal with that same, life-or-death determination. If you think about it, every goal *is* life or death. I've seen a number of people around me die, go to prison, fail, or fuck up their lives with bad choices. They failed to seize an opportunity to change.

I found this posted on the Internet by someone who put things off and didn't seize opportunity: "Today I found out my wife has been cheating on me for the last ten years. My son feels nothing for me. I realized I missed my father's funeral for nothing. I didn't complete my novel, travel the world, or help the homeless. All these things I thought I knew to be a certainty about myself when I was in my late teens and early twenties. If my younger self had met me today, I would have punched myself in the face."

As long as we're breathing, we have the power to make our lives better. The universe has big plans for us as long as we don't hold anything back. We have to define what it is we want and go after it like that lioness stalking her prey. Commit to something, focus all of your time and energy on achieving it, then watch what happens. And if it doesn't happen right away, just stay determined. Like I said in the introduction, sometimes we get tests to check our real desire.

There's a Sanskrit word, *dridha-vrata.* It means "single-minded determination." You must develop *dridha-vrata* and then take action. You want better health? Decide to eat better and exercise and then do it. You want a better career? Do something to make it happen and work your ass off. Want a better relationship? Keep the doors open and make yourself someone you'd want to be with.

Just the other day I saw a young, healthy dude in his mid-twenties nodded out, high on dope, sitting on the sidewalk. His sign read, "Need a miracle. Please spare some change." He doesn't need a miracle. What he needs is a good swift kick in the ass. He needs to get off the drugs, get a job, and stop complaining about how life did him wrong. The choices he himself made daily are what got him to that NYC sidewalk, homeless and strung out, begging for loose change. Shit, even his dirty, hungry pit bull had the look, "Why me, man? Why couldn't I get an owner with a job and a fucking apartment?"

The truth is that the little daily choices we make end up affecting our entire lives. So instead of complaining, "My life sucks. Why is the world against me? My mother didn't hug me enough. Wah, Wah, Wah," do something each day to drive your life to the place you want it to be. Do you know who never complains? Disciplined people. They know nothing changes unless they make it happen. They carve out a path through choice after choice after choice.

I want to tell you about a kid I know named Matt. He lived in the Salvation Army Boys Home on the Bowery some years ago. Some of these kids there come from horrific family situations, as I did, and some are even worse off. One kid's father moved him to NYC from the Dominican Republic, and when he got to the city he murdered his family except for this one kid, leaving him homeless and alone in a new country.

My nephew was in that home as well because things didn't work out with his mom and her asshole boyfriend, so I got to spend a lot of time there and knew a lot of the kids pretty well, even mentoring some of them. Many of the kids acted real tough, trying to play the hard rock role. I recognize it. I've been there. It's a defense mechanism meant to protect them from all the pain and hurt they've endured. Not Matt. He was always kind and polite. It was pretty funny out in public having this 6'5" black teenager calling me Uncle John. Definitely drew some looks.

The Salvation Army afforded each of these kids an opportunity to excel, even to go to college. Matt took advantage of whatever they offered. My nephew and the others chose to be fuck-ups. They made fun of Matt because he stayed out of trouble and worked hard in school. The fuck-ups, well, they played the blame game. It was everyone else's fault they were in trouble. Many, including my nephew, got arrested. Three kids even raped and murdered a woman in the neighborhood and are doing serious time.

Ten years later, my nephew is in jail for the fourth time. Most of the kids in there with him walked down the same path. But do you know who's about to graduate college and has a loving wife and his own apartment? Matt. He seized a golden opportunity when it was in front of him and worked his ass off to get somewhere better in his life. He made something out of nothing and broke the cycle of pain. He avoided negativity even when he was completely surrounded by it. Think about the intestinal fortitude that took for a kid in his circumstances. Talk about peer pressure. Some of those kids could be downright fucking mean, and they were, trust me.

When the deck is stacked against you, you still have to keep yourself in the game.

You have to work so much harder than the next person in order to slay the dragon of the Enemy Mind and your demons of doubt. You have to stay hungry every day to improve your situation. And I'm not talking materialistically hungry. I mean, shit, I'm always giving my possessions away. I'm referring to becoming that single-minded, determined, driven fucker who finishes what he or she starts regardless of the results because he or she knows it's the only way to succeed. You know if you don't get it this time, you can try harder and get a better result in the future.

You have to recognize opportunities and seize them if you want more out of life. The Irish writer Oscar Wilde said, "Discontent is the first step in the progress of a man or a nation." That is pure truth. You have to be dissatisfied and want something better for yourself, your family, or your loved ones in order to move forward. When you get to that place of discontent, you'll figure out how to make it happen and develop the state of mind to succeed. Then you too will go to your corkboard and make your manifest reality.

I've read dozens of articles and books about people who didn't appreciate their lives and took for granted the gift of just opening their eyes every morning and breathing. Then a crisis hits and wakes them the hell up, makes them reevaluate everything.

In the five parts of Story Design—Inciting Incident, Progressive Complications, Crisis, Climax and Resolution—**Crisis** sits dead center. Now, why do you think stories are designed like that? I'll tell you. It's because the crisis is what's needed to drive the character into that last-act climax, where all the most focused antagonists align against him or her. Only in that place will the protagonist choose to take the action to fulfill the desire that sent him or her out there in the first place. That's the resolution.

In life as in any well-written film, the moments we focus on are what's referred to as "the gap between expectation and result." The energy of life is found in that gap. As Robert McKee says in his amazing book *Story,* "A character takes a particular action expecting a result and the universe doesn't cooperate. A gap cracks open and the character must now take a second action to get what he or she wants. This next action puts him or her at risk."

There's that word again—risk. That's life, my friends. We have a view of how we think life should go to make us happy, then life happens and we change our view. I mean, seriously, think about everything you wanted maybe five, ten, or twenty years ago. I know many of my goals have changed. I stayed open to the change. You have to. Diamonds start out as coal, and after millions of years of pressure they become jewels. Then the expert jeweler must chip away the rough cut and create a polished gem.

So what do you want your story to be? Are you the character that fought through gap after gap, accepting greater and greater risk each time in order to achieve your desire? Or are you the character who plays it safe, who never risks? That character will never see the light of day in any of my scripts. Such characters are flat. We don't pay good money at the movies to see flat characters. Shit, we see enough of them in our everyday lives.

You only get the "object of your desire" by acting, by choosing to seize opportunities when they arise, by taking risks. So I challenge you to act by wholeheartedly applying what you're learning in this book, and then tell me you don't feel better about your life, that you didn't develop resilience, a tough skin, a "no quitting or whining" Positive Mental Attitude. You must understand and realize that the only thing standing between you and the life you want is a reluctance to change. That all starts with the ability to recognize, then seize opportunities. Don't make excuses. Never put shit off till tomorrow. Get it done today. List out your object or objects of desire and then crack open those gaps and take action. Seize those opportunities.

Become Resilient

Resilience is defined by most as the ability to recover from setbacks or difficult situations, adapt to change, and keep going in the face of extreme adversity. So why is it that some are able to be resilient while others crumble under pressure?

In my last book, *Meat is For Pussies* (which, by the way isn't only about meat eating), I have a section called "Mental Toughness Training Tips." In it I enlisted the help of some badass men and women, asking them to tell me how they use the mind to push through challenges. I spoke to endurance athletes, combat-experienced Navy SEALs, Army Rangers, high-level martial artists, UFC fighters, and a number of others. In talking with them the one thing I understood was that they were all able to roll with the punches, as we say. If they got knocked down, they didn't let that apparent failure define them. They got up and kept going toward their goal. That's because resilient people don't let adversity define them. They see negative setbacks as temporary.

So how do we develop resilience? I would say the first thing is to remain flexible in how you deal with adversity. No two situations are ever the same, so they demand different approaches or solutions. Say, for example, you get fired. That requires that you first off analyze whether or not it was your fault. If you are at fault, make the necessary changes to your work ethic or character in order to make sure it never happens again.

Next, let's look at the death of a loved one after an illness. That's something you have no control over, of course, but what you can control is how you respond to it. You can let depression set in, start drinking, hit rock bottom, or you can celebrate the person's life by setting up a foundation in his or her name in order to help others. One of my friends showed his resilience when his brother died from cancer. He ran the NYC marathon for his brother—his brother had always wanted to. It was a way to keep his brother in his thoughts and actions. I'll tell you one thing, there wasn't a dry eye around when he posted the event video of himself at the finish line. There are so many things you can do to honor the person and your love for him or her and to remain resilient. Both of these examples will help you develop resilience, but resilience takes constant practice and work.

We have to train the mind to see the positive in the negative. Heidi Reeder, PhD, author of *Commit to Win,* writes, "Research shows that on average, negative events impact people five times as much as positive events do. Resilient people, however, keep the negative from having such a powerful impact by focusing on what's positive in the situation (e.g., "I made a fool of myself in front of the whole team"), or just the upside (e.g., "The team got to see that I am human, which will deepen our relationship"), they are able to hold *both* the positive and negative equally. This kind of emotional balance allows you to move forward with more confidence and less stress."

This is something I practice during my quiet meditation and reflection time—that is, I look back on the tough situations I've had in my life and realize they were in fact a challenge to teach me resilience. All of those situations made me a stronger person. Notice that I practice this in a positive environment, during meditation time, and not when the shit is hitting the fan and I'm in the midst of chaos. By doing it in a positive setting, I'm developing the flexible mental muscles I need to become more resilient.

There are also many lessons in terms of resilience to be learned from our failures.

I actually write later in this book that we must fail in order to succeed. Why? Well, if we reflect on why we failed instead of playing the blame game or flying off the handle, we'll learn to roll with the punches and it will force us to step up our game and develop a thicker skin.

This is why I highly recommend developing a strong fitness routine and getting in shape, which can do wonders for your mental toughness and resilience. Being fit gives you a certain sense of control over challenges that may come up. One of the many things people who are out of shape tell me is that they feel like they've lost control over their bodies. That definitely affects your ability to deal with stress. Being in shape is extremely empowering, and there's much evidence to prove that.

Ben Michaelis, PhD, a New York City psychologist, says, "You can become mentally tougher by becoming physically stronger through cardiovascular exercise. The data indicating the link between physical and emotional health is airtight at this point. This is why I often suggest that people who want to build their emotional resilience begin by strengthening their endurance either through running, which I personally believe (and there is data to support me on this) is the most natural form of exercise for human beings."

That's why resilient people know they have to save energy for themselves no matter what life throws at them on a daily basis. Hectic workload, kids, making their mortgage payments, family problems. Saving energy for yourself is not being self-centered; it's real talk. It goes back to the analogy of the swimmer in rough seas. You have to save yourself first by getting to the boat—then you can help others. By saving energy for *me time*, no matter what that is—swimming, yoga, running, playing music, meditating—you'll put yourself in the best possible state both mentally and physically to deal with challenges when they arise.

As you go through the different sections of this book, you'll discover that the principles are intertwined, some even dependent on each other. Like fitness and resilience, diet and attitude. That's why I constantly stress how important it is to apply all the facets of *The PMA Effect*. I mentioned writing down your goals and pinning them up on your corkboard as a way to visualize them. Do you know what else I write down? Something proven to help people become more resilient—my feelings and emotions. Dr. James Pennebaker writes in his book *Writing to Heal,* "People who engage in expressive writing report feeling happier and less negative than before writing. Similarly, reports of depressive symptoms, rumination, and general anxiety tend to drop in the weeks and months after writing about emotional upheavals."

Writing about yourself isn't narcissistic. You *must* do it. I mean, how do you think this book got started? Every day I was writing down the way certain situations made me feel and how I dealt with them using my PMA practices. I was actually living the book in real life, but everything started with the pen, my friends. It went from my corkboard to my laptop to the printed page. I know I've drilled hard on this quality of resilience, but I have to tell you firsthand that it is the one quality that my upbringing forced me to develop, and it's paying huge dividends to this day.

In closing, I'll leave you with this statement by author and motivational speaker Jean Chatzky: "Resilience isn't a single skill. It's a variety of skills and coping mechanisms. To bounce back from bumps in the road as well as failures, you should focus on emphasizing the positive."

You Must Turn Pro

"Strength and growth come only through continuous effort and struggle."

— *Napoleon Hill*

When I was at boot camp up at Great Lakes Naval Station, they had a motto they drilled into your head from the moment you got there until you graduated: "Attention to detail."

There's a reason the drill instructors make you wear your uniform a certain way, spit-shine your shoes, make your bed precisely with hospital corners, store your gear to perfection, keep your area free of dust, keep groomed to a T, march in unison, turning on a dime, become expert at taking apart your weapon, cleaning it, and reassembling it. It's because they want you to turn pro. Why? In a wartime situation, where it's life and death, the willingness to be a professional will be what you need to work as a team, defeat the enemy, and make it home to your loved ones.

Mediocrity will always give you mediocre results.

It's that slacker recruit who tries to cut corners, who thinks he's getting one over on his instructors, that will be the one who doesn't bring enough ammo to the battlefield and puts his unit in jeopardy. The military teaches you to turn pro, work hard, and play for keeps.

Over the years I've found that the things I've learned in my writing career apply to all areas of my life in that when you make a conscious effort to always do your best, you learn to develop the skillset to improve. You don't just show up, you show up and give it all your energy and focus.

Think about that for a second. What if you tackled every task in your life this way—your job, your career, your training, your spiritual practice, your relationship. Being a hack and faking the funk is a disease that affects many these days. I find that when I fight the desire to cut corners, regardless of whether I'm doing something grand or minute, I become a positive person in other areas of my life as well.

When I'm at the gym, I can see who's really going for it and who's just showing up. That's why there are trainers—to push you out of your comfort zone, your lazy mindset, and to help you achieve results. Good trainers can do that. The other thing is when I see someone in a coffee shop writing a screenplay and texting, talking, checking Facebook—I'm pretty confident that's one script that's not going to make it to the screen.

I am a novice writer, but when I write, it's all social media off, phone off, shit, even my girl knows not to interrupt when I'm in the Lab. I need to focus all of my senses, mind, and intelligence on what I'm doing. Seriously, give it a try. Turn pro. Good things take time to manifest, but if you keep going, you'll get there. It's all about your work ethic. This book is not just some hypothetical read about PMA; it's about developing it, maintaining it, then using it to kick ass every day.

As Steven Pressfield says, "Resistance hates when we turn pro." The follow-up to his bestseller, *The War of Art*, his book *Turning Pro* navigates the passage from amateur to a professional practice.

> **"You don't need to take a course or buy a product. All you have to do is change your mind. Turning pro is free, but it's not easy. When we turn pro, we give up a life that we may have become extremely comfortable with. We give up a self that we have come to identify with and to call our own. Turning pro is free, but it demands sacrifice."**

The fact is, I've watched people who've developed the skillset to turn pro make leaps and bounds in every area of their lives. They pay attention to detail. They take notes and study. They learn the formula, apply it, and get the desired result. If they fail at something, they analyze why, then take the necessary steps to make sure it doesn't happen again. Even in the fight game it's said that a true champion is one who comes back after a loss. He or she goes to the videotape and examines his or her mistakes, then takes action to correct them in the next training camp.

Try it. Develop a new mindset. Everything you do in life, do it for real. Live with purpose. The rapper Big Daddy Kane put it perfectly: "Aint no half steppin'." That's right. There ain't. When you live that way, your entire attitude changes. You will have a light, an aura, about you. People will say things to you like, "Pam, did you lose weight? Did you change your hair? Something's different. What is it?" What's different? Pam turned pro.

I recently heard David Goggins on Rich Roll's podcast. His is one of my favorite episodes. Goggins is a badass former Navy SEAL, the kind of SEAL other SEALs look up to. The shit he has endured to become who he is—holy shit, it's incredible. My buddy is an active-duty frogman. He told me some stories about Goggins that blew me the eff away. Well, one of the things Goggins expresses in that podcast is his view that mediocrity is destroying America and that many people don't want to be told the truth, so they surround themselves with enablers.

David Goggins got to where he is by confronting the dark secrets and fears not many are willing to admit. I'm fat, I'm lazy, I'm a liar. Nowadays, everyone gets a trophy. We celebrate defeat and choose friends that never call us out on our bullshit. Instead, they tell us, "Don't worry, John, let it go. You'll get 'em next time." No,

I won't. Unless I change my mindset, analyze, figure it out—if I don't turn pro—I'll keep coming up short time after time.

I'll get into why failing is important in the next section.

Developing a hack's mindset works against your turning pro. It makes you complacent. It stops your self-improvement. It destroys your PMA.

And God forbid you try to call people out on it in a world where everyone is so easily offended. I agree 100 percent with David on this. That crap-ass attitude is destroying the minds of people in this country. These days, when you tell someone the truth, they get the "poopie-pants attitude and kick rocks," as Mr. Goggins says. But in his line of work, people who don't turn pro die.

It's a little different in the civilian world, of course, but death is still a possibility. Case in point: if my real friends didn't call me out on my bullshit, I'd be dead. I know plenty who have died because no one stepped up, no one intervened. I come from a much different time. Had I got butt-hurt back then because people told me I was full of shit, I wouldn't be here now. I most certainly wouldn't be writing this book.

I had zero self-worth coming out of my childhood, but I refused to let that be my story. If I'd let that define me, the bastards who did all that fucked-up shit to me as a kid would have won. I made a lot of mistakes, some I'm still paying for, but I was never afraid to fail or so afraid of what others thought that I got paralyzed and took no action. Shit, all I ever knew was failure. It came to a point in lockup where I was so frustrated with my life that I threw up my hands and prayed. Krishna sent answers my way, but it was still up to me to make a decision and act on it.

Do you know what I did? I hung around with top-tier human beings doing positive things and I studied how they lived and tackled the obstacles in their lives. Then I took action. Sure, maybe I was mimicking at first, but when I rolled up my sleeves, when I said I'm tired of mediocrity, when I tried to figure out this PMA thing by changing my mindset and turning pro, well, that's when things started to happen. It can happen for you too. I guarantee it with 100 percent certainty. All that's required is that you *change your mindset and turn pro*!

Those Who Fail/Succeed

"Before success comes in any man's life, he's sure to meet with much temporary defeat and, perhaps some failures. When defeat overtakes a man, the easiest and the most logical thing to do is to quit. That's exactly what the majority of men do."

—Napoleon Hill

Fear of failure paralyzes some people, doesn't it? The reason is they're too attached to the end result instead of enjoying the ride. They can never be present in the moment because they're caught up in "what if." What if it all goes wrong? What if this or that happens?

Personally, I learned to simply enjoy the challenge and be present for it, in the moment. If I were to sit and overanalyze things I would never even get started. So many people I know fall victim to this. They worry what everyone will think if their effort doesn't bring the best result.

Now, on the surface, this may seem counterintuitive. I said earlier that we have to act for the love of doing the thing and not for the result. Why should we be detached from the result? I mean, shit, you even refer to success in the damn title of your book, John. But the question we have to ask ourselves right out of the box is why am I even *doing* a particular thing? What's my motivation?

> **When the only reason we're doing something is to stroke our ego—because we're hoping for fame, adoration, and distinction—then we have the wrong mindset.**

After we finish that race, book, script or whatever the case may be, when the numbers are all in, then it's okay to want to improve. You must.

Another one of the dirty little tricks the Enemy Mind uses to con us is expecting perfection right out of the box. That's a mistake the amateur makes, and one that will eventually lead you to give up. I mean, sure, some of you may be able to write an Academy Award-winning screenplay in one month, but my guess is that the rest of us have to fail and fail and fail before we learn enough to get it right. Many times the results won't match our expectations, so learn to love the *entire* journey—the good, the bad, and the ugly, as well as the eventual success.

In November 2014 I went to race Ironman Florida in Panama City. I got down there four days before the race began and the weather was great—mid-seventies, gentle breezes, a calm ocean. Then as if the weather gods were punishing me, race day was thirty-nine degrees, steady, forty mph winds, high seas, and a very bad riptide. The Ironman water safety team canceled the swim even as I stood there in my wetsuit. It was now only bike and run. To make matters worse, I had failed to prepare and had no cold-weather gear. I raced in a compression tank top and shorts.

I finished the 112-mile bike ride and was freezing. As I stepped into the changing tent (T2), I thought, "Should I take twenty minutes to run to the hotel to grab a sweatshirt and sweatpants?" I decided I'd warm up while I was running. I was dead wrong. The wind picked up and the temperature dropped. Thirteen miles in I was hypothermic. My hands were blue. I was vomiting. I went into a Porta Potty (filled with all that loveliness) to try to warm up, but it started spinning. I actually had to put both hands on the wall to stop from falling over. Then more vomiting and trembling with shivers. I got out and called it a day after the medical team suggested I do so. I was toast. Felt like shit. I was beat up both mentally and physically. I went back to the hotel, which was close to the finish line, and had to listen as they called out the names of the people who had made it: "Bob Smith—you are an Ironman!" My Enemy Mind said, "No they ain't. There was no swim." But you know what? They toughed it out and I didn't—so fuck my bullshit attitude. They get props.

The next day I hit rock bottom. I had to pull myself out of my shit, and to do that I needed advice from friends who'd accomplished incredible things while staring down adversity. One of the first people I contacted was my boy—that decorated Navy SEAL who was in the film *Act of Valor*. He was deployed in the Middle East, facing life and death, and yet he took the time out to help a friend. He pulled no punches. This is what he wrote me, verbatim: "John, inherently, humans want to know what it takes to get the job done. PMA, proper preparation, etc., all play a major role. If you plant any seeds of doubt at all, it will totally start crushing your foundation. Fortify your mind; don't allow it to happen. Don't sweat it, bruddah. Come back stronger next time; use this failure as a steppingstone."

Now, when a man of that character and integrity gives you advice, you had better listen and listen good. The truth is, I've seen shit way worse than this and made it through. My life has been constant obstacles and I have overcome every single one of them.

Actually, my lady said she didn't realize Florida was such a big letdown for me because I never let on what I was going through. That's because I'm a master at concealing pain. It comes from my childhood. I never wanted to show weakness or vulnerability. When horrible things were happening to me, I never let on. No matter what, I didn't let those bastards win by showing them that they hurt me. That ability to hide pain is something I still need to work on, but as I said, I'm a work in progress. With PMA, though, I know that I will get there eventually if I walk the walk.

And speaking of walking the walk, after I stopped feeling sorry for myself and brooding like a chump, I got my head out of my ass and realized there's a pattern to all this. I've seen it time and again—failure resulting in growth. I fell back on what got me through all the hard times: focusing on small, positive things I can actively do every day to dig myself out of the mental trenches. I gave no time for the idle mind—definitely the devil's workshop. I went for a two-mile pool swim. I hit the gym. I biked. I ran. I wrote. I always write—that's my therapy. I wrote about what I was going through and it helped me heal. I started smiling and feeling great.

A few days later I turned on my computer and there was an email from the Ironman website. "Still slots available for Cozumel Ironman November 30th. Sign up now!" Right away the Enemy Mind immediately attacked. "What if you fail, John? Then you'll really be the laughingstock. Remember Florida? You'll feel ten times worse. You haven't even been training as hard. Don't do it, John!" I cursed that fucker and hit the **Register Now** tab!

I had two weeks until race time and so started training like a madman. I told no one except my girl. The fact is, no one needed to know. This was *my* mission, and it was top secret. I needed redemption, and for that I had to dig deep. 2014 had stacked major adversity on my plate: a family tragedy, career setbacks, a torn calf muscle earlier in the year, having to pull out of Ironman Cabos and Texas. I was tested on every level conceivable. That being said, I could not and would not let 2014 go out on a sour note.

Most of the time it's not adversity that breaks us but how we deal with it. It's our response that determines success or failure. The power of positive thinking can pull us out of anything if we're willing to invest in changing our future. If I want tomorrow to kick ass, I have to get my butt in gear today, not make resolutions to start in the future. Most New Year's Eve resolutions don't last even a month. There's no future; there's only today. If you think like this, you'll never put anything off.

So after all that had happened, I knew I needed to dig deep. I had to beat my mind with a stick every day and stay focused, not wasting even a minute. I mean, shit, in two weeks I would be flying to a foreign country, getting into the ocean and swimming 2.4 miles, biking 112, and then running a 26.2-mile marathon. There was no room for mental demons. Not now. I wrote my training regimen on index cards, pinned them to my corkboard, and got busy. I went to Cozumel and finished, setting a new PR (personal record).

The truth is, the more failures we face, the more we learn from them, thereby increasing our chance at success. Experiencing failure means you pushed through, persisted, kept going. The human quality to be resilient is the capacity to quickly recover in strength and spirits after difficulty; it's mental toughness. Being resilient will allow us to happy in the long run. I've seen this firsthand. People who are resilient are some of the happiest people I know. They never get depressed. It's a quality I've worked hard to develop over the years, and it has helped me beat down my inner demons.

It's not enough to be passionate. You've got to want something so badly that you are uncomfortable when you're not getting it.

Starve yourself and witness firsthand what hunger pangs are. When you feel that kind of hunger to get your shit done, you won't quit and you'll always do your best. My many failures and the hunger that resulted from them, the drive to improve, have molded me into the person I am today. I've made mistakes when things were at the highest risk possible—namely life and death or a very long prison sentence. Truth be told, I was scared straight. I wanted more out of life, so I took the necessary actions to make that happen.

Don't get complacent and comfortable. That's a death sentence. You can grow or you can die. When there's something in life to fall back on—a safety net in the form of parents or significant other or friends or a trust fund—then it's easy to be comfortable. I never had any of that, so I knew if I didn't get out there and work my ass off, I wasn't going to eat or have a place to live. I've stayed hungry, and that hunger drove me to push through my many failures. Failing to succeed is all part of the game.

So don't sit around worrying what your critics will say. You know what I say? Fuck the critics. The world is full of them. Most are failures who themselves gave up and then turned their anger against those who try. Just keep going. If you have passion and a hunger to improve, you'll get there even if you fail. Remember:

slipping up and giving up are two different things. The critic only wins if you give up. So don't. Prove them wrong.

Dig this amazing quote from Theodore Roosevelt: "It is not the critic who counts; not the man who points out how the strong man stumbles, or where the doer of deeds could have done them better. The credit belongs to the man who is actually in the arena, whose face is marred by dust and sweat and blood, who strives valiantly; who errs and comes short again and again; because there is not effort without error and shortcomings; but who does actually strive to do the deed; who knows the great enthusiasm, the great devotion, who spends himself in a worthy cause, who at the best knows in the end the triumph of high achievement and who at the worst, if he fails, at least he fails while daring greatly. So that his place shall never be with those cold and timid souls who know neither victory nor defeat."

Simple Living & High Thinking

I'm going to hip you to something: having a lot of shit won't make you happy. If it did, rich people wouldn't be on all those meds for depression. The fact of the matter is that whenever we look outside ourselves for happiness by overconsuming, we can know that we've missed the boat to happiness.

Here's an analogy. What if you had a car but cared only for its exterior, never maintaining the engine or any of its vital innards? Not too smart, right? Actually, it's downright dangerous. Well, that's where most of society is at these days. They're running around like crazy people, senses out of control, consuming everything, looking for some sort of artificial happiness. Because of it we've become the most depressed, overmedicated, unhealthy people to ever inhabit the earth. The key to happiness is to slow down and take inventory of your internal life, not your bank account and your crap.

This isn't religion I'm talking here. Religion tells you what to do and sometimes encourages blind following. That's just fanaticism. The path I follow is one of deep understanding and knowledge—knowledge that tells you who you are and then let's you decide for yourself what to do about it. In Sanskrit, the phrase *athato brahma jijnasa* means, "Now is the time to inquire about self-realization." To understand how to live, how to be happy, how to always have PMA—all that can only be attained when we're in our constitutional position, or as I wrote in the Cro-Mag song, when we're "Seekers of the Truth."

You can't buy your way out of the blues. We're not born happy; happiness comes through our unique set of experiences and how we choose to respond to them. I've experienced more happiness meditating and chanting at sunrise than chasing down some materialistic mirage.

So many people get caught up in what I call the "item syndrome" that they forget what truly makes us happy. So, sure, the new I-Phone X or Call of Duty game you slept outside Best Buy to get will make you feel good for a few days, but both the iPhone and the game—and your high from owning them—are temporary. The nature of anything nonpermanent is it causes hankering and lamentation. You hanker for something, you get it, and after a while you're dissatisfied and off chasing the next mirage. It's called the law of diminishing returns. That first piece of cake makes you ecstatic, but by the sixth you fucking puke.

I see this big time with the youth these days. They have been so overstimulated by gadgets and materialism that they have no idea what will truly make them happy. I can tell you right now that the pharmaceutical companies are just rubbing their greedy, fucking palms together waiting to fill those prescriptions for depression meds down the road.

There's an Indian story about a holy man who turned away from his spiritual path and became addicted to sex with a prostitute. He would do anything to see her, risking even his own life, because she lived in a dangerous area full of murdering thieves. One day, during the rainy season, a fierce storm blew up and flooded the fields. The man was scheduled to see her that night, so despite the heavy rain he headed out. To get to her house he had to cross a usually shallow river. This night, though, he was swept up in the raging water and nearly drowned. He managed to grab on to what he thought was a tree log and managed to get across. When he got to the other side, however, he realized he'd been holding onto a dead body.

Thieves robbed and beat him severely before he made it to her door. He showed up at her place bloodied but still wanting to enjoy her. The prostitute, who was actually a devotee said, "If you dedicated even one drop of the desire you have to enjoy me to your yoga practice, you'd be a self-realized soul by now." Hearing that snapped the man out of his illusion, and he thanked her and returned home, where he lived out the rest of his life on the path of self-realization.

Do you see the point? We're driven like hell to acquire so much temporary nonsense and bullshit, things that mean absolutely nothing in the scope of permanence and what's real. Simple living and high thinking are key to a fulfilling life. I mean, shit, look around at the people of America. We have overcomplicated our lives to the max. We've become so materialistic. We have everything we want, but it's still never enough. Cars, smart phones, big screen, hi-def TVs, cash, bling, video games—gadget after gadget. None of it will ever satisfy us, because we're spiritual by nature. There will always be a void when chasing the mirage of materialistic life. There will always be hankering, then lamentation, because we're not satisfied. Then we go chasing the next mirage, which again leaves us bone-dry thirsty.

The most peaceful, stress-free time of my life was when I renounced everything and lived as a monk for nearly three years. So much superfluous bullshit clutters the lives of people in America and the other economically advanced countries around the world. And don't get it twisted: poverty in the United States, Western Europe, Australia, and other first-world countries is nothing like third-world poverty. Just go to India or countries in Africa to have your eyes opened on that—and yet in those places you see so many happy, smiling faces.

So here's my challenge: take the same drive, determination, and energy you have for enjoying nonsense and direct it toward positive endeavors of a higher, internal nature. I'm telling you right now, if you can even do a little of that, things will begin to turn around for you. Every journey starts with a first step. Just take a few little ones—baby steps, if you will. I mean, what do you have to lose?

That's why when people tell me, "Things just ain't happening for me, John," I sit them down and make them analyze, take inventory, of what they're doing day to day. How do they spend their time—every waking minute? Do they take the steps necessary to get what they want, or do they half-ass it? Are they hacks or do they give their projects 100 percent of their undivided attention, put their hearts and souls into them, hold nothing back.

You see, often, therein lies the problem. It's not about what you're giving but what you're holding back. It's all based on desire, and had you better be all in if you honestly expect to get anywhere in this world. That I know for sure. I had no silver spoon. I had to claw my way out of the depths of hell to achieve anything I have. Many of you might be in hell now. Fight on and don't stop.

People chase temporary illusions, lusting for one thing after another only to find repeated disappointment. There's a phrase in the Bhagavad Gita where Krishna and Arjuna are talking about lust for matter. Krishna tells Arjuna that this lust is *dush-puren-analena cha:* "It burns like fire and is never satisfied." If you want real satisfaction, keep your life simple and search for meaning. In his best-selling book *The Purpose-Driven Life,* Rick Warren urges us to ask ourselves why we're here. What's our purpose? I'd like to add to those questions, "Where am I going?" I mean, seriously. Am I supposed to wander through life ignorant of my internal life, simply chasing mirages as I try to satisfy my external shell?

I have to mention that there are, of course, those who feel the need to criticize people who have chosen some type of spiritual path. They say, "When you die, it's over, so why bother?" First, that's not true. Just talk to anyone who's had a near-death experience where he or she stood outside the body, or people who go to the house they lived in in a previous life and recognize it, or children of two or three able to play Mozart. Second, yes, I don't necessarily know what's coming after, but guess what, homie, I'm happy in the here and now. So while you're content to believe we're nothing but a collection of molecules, I have a daily practice that brings me happiness and PMA. It seems most of the ones denying the existence of a Higher Power are pretty miserable sons-a-bitches.

We get a human body after many evolutionary births in this world. We get it to facilitate self-realization. The ability to see ourselves in truth is what separates us from the animals that simply seek sense satisfaction. Eating, sleeping, mating, and defending—think about it: it's what animals do with their days. But if you think a little further, animals have souls too; they're not machines. Look in your dog's eyes and tell me it has no soul. So if your only shot in life was to be born a dog, or worse, a dog in India with mange, don't you think you got cheated?

Only in the human form of life do we seek out higher knowledge of a metaphysical nature. This is because there is a code stamped into our soul's DNA, where our inherent nature is, called *ananda, bliss.* It's right next to another code called *sat,* "truth." *Sat* also means "eternal." We're wired to want a happiness that doesn't die. By contact with the material body we suffer. The more we identify ourselves with the body and other forms of matter, and so try to enjoy all that temporary stuff, the more we'll come up short.

Renunciation and *sadhana* (spiritual practice) have their rewards. There are amazing levels of happiness and bliss to be found in the realm of spirit.

Otherwise, how could monks or those living lives of austerity carry on? It's not artificial. Faith takes you a lot of the way, but you also need *rasa,* a life filled with flavor. Our nature is to enjoy. Living artificially can only take you so far. Even me—when I was a monk I was the happiest I've ever been in my life, without question. The problem came when I eased up on my daily practice. Then the Enemy Mind attacked.

The trick is, don't get caught up with and attached to all this stuff. Money can't buy you love, and it certainly can't get you a ticket out of this material world. So put down the remote, X Box control, cell phone, and credit card, and go out and experience the world. There are so many things you could be doing to enrich your life that doesn't involve buying shit.

I read a story a while back about a guy who made millions in the tech industry. He was always stressed out and miserable, which eventually helped him develop a disease that almost killed him. While he was in the hospital, he talked to a man in the next bed who was dying of cancer. He was amazed at how happy this man was. He asked, "How can you be so happy when you're about to die?" The man replied, "I am not about to die, I'm just giving up my bodily dress. I'll change my clothes the way we each change our clothes every day. We're all dying all the time. Where is your two-year-old body or your twenty-year-old body? Everyone born will eventually be faced with what I'm facing, whether it comes in the form of cancer, old age, or an accident. Death is guaranteed. For one who is born, death is certain. What's not certain is whether or not we'll be happy while we're alive. Besides, the truth is, even if I had your millions, these doctors could still do nothing for me. I'm content with my situation and have faced it. I am not afraid because all I have to lose is this temporary, external shell of a body."

That man left his body fearlessly because he'd lived a simple life and thought highly and deeply. Yoga, meditation, higher thought—he practiced all this daily. That brought him realizations, not speculations. Being an armchair philosopher doesn't get you there. You have to put in the work, take action, and live the life if you want the reward. Open that jar of maple syrup and taste the sweetness it contains.

The tech dude listening to this man's story survived and vowed to change. When he got out of the hospital, he gave away his stuff—the cars and houses—and donated most of his wealth to charity. He then moved into a studio apartment, took up yoga and meditation, and stopped eating poisonous foods. He even started running marathons. He lived life to the fullest and was blissed-out because of it. He told the reporters he would never go back to the way he was before.

The man who passed away was in fact a messenger who arrived at the right moment in this dude's life. He told him to stop stressing over what will be and live life in the here and now. The illusion that more money will solve your issues and make you happy down the road is just that, an illusion. It's like getting a postdated check you can't cash. It will just never bring happiness.

If life's about a set of experiences, go get those experiences. Keep your life simple. Keep it highly motivated by switching your thought process to a higher frequency, a higher level of consciousness.

I can only tell you what's worked for me as well as others I know. We've all been in our mental and physical hells. That's the nature of this material world. It's designed to be hell so that we'll want to get out. My guru Srila Prabhupada compared the world to a toilet: not a place you want to linger, have a snack, plan out your life. No. You do your business and get the hell out. The truth is, most suffering and fear we experience is due only to ignorance. It can and will change if you make a plan to live more spiritually, keep it simple, and put in the work day after day.

And let's be clear on a very important point here: just because you live simply doesn't mean you shouldn't try and become successful and make money. Money is energy, and you need it for almost anything in this world. It's an energy you can use for good or for bad. With the albeit limited amount of money I've made, I've been able to do some amazing things. I've fed the homeless, opened a center that taught free bhakti yoga classes, and helped many in need. I know I have to continue to do the work because I want to continue my philanthropic endeavors, to use my income to help others. I put those goals on my corkboard too, by the way.

A man recently asked me what the catalyst was for my change. I replied that somehow I had had enough sense to know that acquiring material shit wasn't going to make me happy, but I was frustrated and suffering like hell, mentally. I knew I had to change or die (or be in prison for the rest of my life), because my anger and drug use was way out of control. I remember not even knowing how to pray or who to pray to, but I prayed anyway. I asked for a roadmap out of my suffering and it came in the form of *jnana*, knowledge, which I then applied. Guess what happened? Change.

I'd been beaten up by the material energy long enough. I wanted sweet things to come into my life. So I stopped speculating on what could be and cracked open that jar of maple syrup. I took action. I lived a simple life, I meditated and worked my ass off. Change can come for anyone who wants it. It doesn't come cheap, but the rewards are immeasurable. I'm no different from any of you. You'll get there too if you're willing to walk the walk.

Give it a try and I can guarantee you amazing things will come to your life. When they do, don't forget to pay it forward and to help others. That's what *The PMA Effect* is all about.

What Goes Around Comes Around

Why is it that we admire philanthropists so much—those who give to others out of the goodness of their hearts, expecting nothing in return? What have they figured out that the rest of the world needs to catch up on?

I'll tell you. They know that by helping others they become happy. Aesop wrote, "No act of kindness, no matter how small, is ever wasted." It's not that we have to open a hospital or donate millions of dollars to help others. We can start simply, from where we're at, from a place where we have facility. That could even be something as small as offering kind words of encouragement to someone going through hard times.

We should always be happy when others do well. Shit, I am. When I see my friends get a movie deal, book deal, finish an album, complete some amazing physical challenge, lose fifty pounds, finish a race, start to eat plant-based, quit smoking, win an MMA fight—or *whatever*—it brings a smile to my face.

I'm bringing this up for a specific purpose.

In my years on this planet I've noticed that those who help and encourage others are some of the happiest people I've ever met. They exude PMA—matter of fact, it's dripping out of every cell in their body.

Ever since I learned about the world of cause and effect (karma), I've made a conscience effort to help others in an attempt to fix my own screwed-up life and to change my negative attitude to a positive one. I've discovered that when I put good works out into the world, I become much happier.

Then there's the dark side of humanity, those who go out of their way to harm others. They take joy in seeing others in pain. Sometimes they even try to add fuel to the fire by causing them more pain. These people are envious and critical of anything someone else earned by hard work. They are faultfinders. Like flies, they're constantly looking for piles of shit. I've personally known and still know some of these types, and I make a conscious effort to get far the hell away from them and keep it that way.

Before reading Don Ruiz's *The Four Agreements,* when people talked crap or spread lies, I straight up wanted to beat the shit out of them. Then I got *Agreements.* One of the agreements is "Don't take things personally." Understand that a person in hellish consciousness and a negative world can never have anything good to say or any kind act to perform. Such persons live only to harm others and ultimately themselves through their choices.

Unlike those who have PMA, envy, anger, and negativity are found in every cell of their bodies. Those people can never be happy. Compassion and caring are qualities that enliven the soul because they are our essence. But envy is the worst quality imaginable because it takes people to very dark places, places consumed by hate. Envy is the root of all evil; envious people always try to harm others. Thus the expression, "an envious snake." Did you know that cobras have been known to climb trees just before they die just so they can drop on someone (or something) and get in that last deadly bite? Envious people are no different, with their snakelike mentalities.

Causing someone mental or emotional stress is, in many ways, worse than punching them in the face. The pain of a punch only lasts a day or two. Emotional pain can last for years. I'm always looking for ways to help others out of painful situations. To see others suffering and unhappy makes me unhappy. Being instrumental in helping them turn things around fulfills a deep need in me, because I've been where they are and can relate. You, too, should practice this compassion code.

And you don't just get bad karma for hurting other *people;* you also get it for the cruelty in your diet. You need to ask yourself at every meal, "What effect am I having on other living beings by eating this?" I mean, think about what an animal has to go through to make you that hamburger, pork chop, chicken wing, slice of bacon, or steak: a life of hellish confinement and torture, followed by being violently murdered. Do you really want to consume that energy? Why do you think they transport animals at night and that there are no guided tours of slaughterhouses? Believe me, they know if people got to see what's being done to the animals that feed them—if they witnessed the animal holocaust—they'd go veg in a second.

I suggest you don't stick your head in the sand anymore about that. Live consciously. Go visit a CAFO (Concentrated Animal Feeding Operation), where upwards of a hundred thousand animals are crammed together and fattened for slaughter. If the smell doesn't make you puke and turn you off, take another step further and go into a slaughterhouse. Unless you're a sick, twisted fucker, I can guarantee you'll be deeply affected.

On the subway recently, I saw someone take a few bites out of a hamburger and then just toss it. For some reason it got to me. Now, I'm not one to scream at people who are wearing furs or even go out and protest about animal rights, for that matter, but I felt compelled to say something to this girl. I broke it down for her, informing her what that animal had endured throughout its life to become that Big Mac. I kept my cool, though, dropping logic and science, and who knows if I got through to her. But I like to think she checked out the doc films and websites I suggested.

When we harm others, whether humans, animals, birds, or fish, you had better believe there is karma involved. Being nonviolent doesn't mean you sit back, become a pacifist and let people walk all over you and your loved ones. Oh, hell no. Real warriors are strong enough to only use force when necessary. Actually a very high-level black belt told me that just the other day. He does everything he can to avoid physical confrontation, but if there's no other solution, he must use force—he has no problem with it.

In closing, I'll tell you one thing I am certain of because I lived it. PMA doesn't come by accident, by chance. It grows out of the actions we perform every single day. Living a life of ahimsa, non-violence, toward every living being, especially those we've wrongly considered food, will fast-track your PMA. Trust me, practicing ahimsa won't make you weak. It will make you strong, *very* strong, in fact. So put some good karma in that bank account, get out there, and go kick some ass.

Act Like a Child

"A great man never ignores the simplicity of a child."

— *Chinese proverb*

First off, don't get it twisted here, I don't mean *childish,* like someone who always has to get his way, complaining, pouting stomping feet to get attention, a big baby—those pain-in-the-ass people annoy the living hell out of me. What I'm referring to is staying open to dream of life's amazing possibilities.

If you ask children what they want to be when they grow up, they'll tell you anything from an astronaut to a football player to the president. Nothing's off the table or feels unattainable to them. Do you know what you'll never hear a kid say? "I'm just going to give up on my dreams, live a boring existence, and drag my ass to a dead-end job I hate, then drink away my sorrows."

As life goes on, we adults tend to become safely hidden in our comfort zones. We become conditioned, set in limited ways of doing things, and we lose our flexibility and the ability to try new paths. We think we already have it figured out and that no one can tell us anything. We tend to stagnate in all aspects of life—career, relationships, or spiritual advancement. Our conditioning programs us to believe the self-defeating statements we have created for ourselves: I'm not talented enough. I'm not creative enough. I'm not young enough, not gifted, smart, pretty, skinny, or handsome enough. These are all lies, and to change our path we must change our perspective.

Have you ever watched kids play? They totally commit to whatever they're doing. They stay in the moment. Unlike adults they aren't thinking about later, tonight, tomorrow, or next week. They use all of their imagination to get lost in their world of make-believe for hours on end, and they want to make their dreams a reality. Children take risks. There's no fear of failure. Because of that, self-condemnation eludes them. They act without worrying about the results or who's watching or judging them.

Kids usually take their time. They don't care that society says they have to act a certain way. They aren't afraid to break the rules in order to create. They stay unpredictable. Children are designed to be great learners. It's dialed into their DNA to be constantly gaining new knowledge and insights, and most will accept new ways of doing things. They ask questions free from embarrassment.

When I hit fifty but continued playing music, touring, writing books, films, and racing Ironman triathlons, some people my age criticized me: "How long are you gonna keep living in some fantasy, John? When are you gonna get serious about life?" Actually, I'm dead fucking serious about life. That's why I try to live it to the fullest every day, to give it my all, to be all in and go for it, to see every endeavor through to the end, to dream like a kid, knowing full well that all my hard work will pay off.

Actually, that type of criticism comes from those who have themselves given up, who've become content to live out their quiet lives of desperation. It's why they feel the need to try to convince everyone around them to do the same. Point blank, those people suck. What they spew is poisonous to your PMA and your personal growth. Don't ever accept what they say as fact. A real friend will always encourage you to go for your dreams, help you get into the mindset that you can do anything and everything. Real friends never try to sow seeds of doubt. You must reject those who do.

When you stop questioning, dreaming and learning like children, it's a type of soul death. You become a cog in the machine satisfied simply to exist. Imagine if all the great writers, poets, actors, philosophers, athletes, musicians, philanthropists, and so many others listened to people who told them to quit. Risk-takers are the ones who get shit done. And most risk-takers I know have the same mentality in their work as children do in their play.

Business speaker and best-selling author Jack Uldrich writes, "When people think the way children do they begin to see things from a new perspective, they learn to step back and view problems, people, and things from a completely different point of view."

For the most part, children are happy and don't get depressed—or if they do, they don't tend to stay depressed for long. Shit, even when I was being abused on a daily basis in that foster home, I still found ways to smile and be happy. I created other worlds. I played. I dreamed and fantasized about being a musician. As a result I became resilient, determined, and gained the strength to get me through things. Oh, yeah, and I became a musician who tours to this day!

Only as children grow to adulthood do negative traits manifest and take over. It's because we believed the doubters and stopped listening to our inner child. We caved and gave up on dreams and goals. This section is an important one in terms of developing PMA and happiness.

Stay childlike and approach everything you do with the eyes of a child.

Here I am, about to turn 56, and I just wrote a new album, two new books, a feature film, a TV series, and I'm also still touring and competing in Ironman triathlons. Do I ever sit there, thinking, "What if my movie never gets made? What if my album isn't received well? What if I don't finish the race?" Hell, no! I love the act, and like a child I'm free from doubt. I never listen to those who are spreading the seeds of poison. I always believe that anything and everything is possible if I'm willing to remain creative, work my ass off, and think outside the box.

You must think like this as well. It's your calling in life. You are meant for greatness. You have unlimited potential and the power to create amazing things, to live life to the utmost, and to love unlimitedly. That's real talk. If you don't believe what I'm saying here, go and eavesdrop on some kids' conversation while they're playing. I guarantee you'll learn a whole lot from it.

Exercise:

Try something new. Don't worry about the results; just act. Learn to play an instrument. Try yoga or meditation. Take a creative writing course. Learn a new language. Get involved with a theater company. Start a band for fun with friends. Join a recreational sports league or take up a hobby. Grow an organic vegetable garden. What it is doesn't matter. Each of these will exercise your mind. As a result, you'll grow. In all that you do, just remember to do it with the simplicity and carefree attitude of a child.

Find That Higher Power

My intention in this section is not to preach or convince you to follow one path over another but to simply present certain undeniable truths and then let you make your way through them.

That's what I've done in my life. It has taken decades to get to where I'm at, and I still have a long way to go. What I've learned and accepted as my truth has come from my own set of unique experiences.

That being said, how could I ever tell someone else what to believe? People who do that are the biggest fools. And to follow blindly is ludicrous. That's why I believe that the major religions have failed people. People are more dissatisfied with organized religion than ever, and not just because of hypocrisy among some of the leaders, either.

The disappointment comes because most large religious groups have to be so rule-based that they tend to attract fanatic or fundamentalist followers as their lowest common denominator. Fundamentalists, by definition, have little or no philosophical understanding about why their religion does what it does, and for them, the enemy is not the uncontrolled mind but those who disagree with their idea of religion. If you were to ask them why they do certain things, they don't say, "Because I meditated on it for years and dug to the core of my existence, searching for answers. This is what I came up with." Instead they say they're following their priest or pastor or guru from India. Spiritual practice without philosophy is fanaticism. And philosophy without devotion is mental concoction and speculation. You need both, devotion and philosophy.

What I can tell you for sure: if you are truly on a search for truth, you will find it. You will discover your path to your Higher Power. Perhaps your Higher Power is the belief that you should serve others.

I have the utmost respect for those who give aid to others. It's our nature to serve. Just as you can't separate heat and light from fire, you can't separate the desire to be of service from the living entity. As Bob Dylan says, "You gotta serve somebody." Whether you serve God, country, your husband or wife, your kids, your dog, or your senses, one way or other you serve.

We are all energy. That energy is of a divine nature. We belong to a great collective that joins all life together. We are stronger together. One stick alone can be snapped, and alone, so can we. But when we link to the collective consciousness, we're like a bundle of sticks that cannot be broken. You see this even in the mundane sense, with people joining this or that group so they can hang around with people who have common interests. Why shouldn't we do the same on the road to PMA and higher consciousness? Remember, we're meant for teamwork.

You can be part of the darkness or part of the light, part of the problem or part of the solution. We don't come into this world with any labels attached; labels get assigned—and we assign them to others—as we become socially conditioned. Most religions teach "My God is better than yours." Most societies teach "My race is better than yours." Sexism—men are superior to women. All of that is ignorance. It's not of a higher nature but a lower frequency, because in truth, our essence is not black or white, man or woman, or of any particular religion—not Christian, Hindu, Muslim, or Jew. These are all temporary labels. What we are is of a divine, spiritual nature. That truth is called **sanatana-dharma,** or universal, eternal truth. Our only occupation is service, and that service has to be unconditional, unmotivated, uninterrupted, and loving. The real love of the soul isn't motivated by expectations of what we're going to get out it.

If you stand in front of a very dusty mirror, you won't be able to see your image reflected. But as soon as you clear away the dust, you'll see who you are. It's the same on the path of truth. Working on ourselves clears the dust, and gradually we see more and more reflected in that mirror. You'll see all people as brothers and sisters, animals as friends we should protect, and Mother Earth the mother we should respect and care for.

Now, look around this Age of Kali, of quarrel and hypocrisy. Everything is ass-backwards. We fight over anything, kill hundreds of billions of animals every year, and destroy the hell out of the planet. This cannot continue if we ever expect to live in peace. I can only refer to what I know as my truth. When I searched, meditated, and worked hard, I found my Higher Power. I wasn't following blindly, as many who don't believe in a Higher Power suggest; rather, it was through working on myself enough that I began to get deeper insights and a more philosophical understanding of what was going on around me.

We all want to feel connected to something bigger than ourselves, but if we disconnect from the power source, we'll eventually run out of power. It doesn't matter what you call your Higher Power, you must reach outside yourself. And believe me, I've heard all the arguments: "You're accepting something you can't see," and all the rest. You can't see cell phone or satellite TV signals, but you have faith that when you turn on your iPhone or TV you'll be able to talk, text, or watch your program. People have faith in all kinds of things. They exit their houses with the faith that they'll return safely to their families. Yet when you say you have faith in a Higher Power, there are some who will immediately criticize or disparage.

So yes, through our mundane vision we may not be able to see everything that's there. Our physical senses are imperfect. But if we develop spiritual vision, we'll know how to find our Higher Power. We'll discover higher frequencies, different planes of existence beyond this mundane world of matter and illusion.

Finding that Higher Power should be the ultimate goal of everyone who's reading this book. PMA is important and an integral part of the process, but it's not the end. It's simply a tool you'll need in your arsenal as you travel toward self-awareness, enlightenment, and true happiness.

Shhh... It's a *Secret*

Okay, I'm calling out all these snake oil salesmen and women making millions off their new-age crap, because the secret's out, and that is—it ain't no secret! So don't buy into their bullshit. *You* have to take charge of your own life. *You* create your destiny by *your* daily actions.

Now, I'm not saying you don't need teachers. I've already discussed the need of mentors. What I *am* saying is that when there's a hefty price tag accompanying knowledge of how to work on yourself, look out.

My spiritual teacher, my guru, Srila Prabhupada, gave his knowledge away for **FREE**. He never charged one thin dime. Morning classes were also followed by a sumptuous breakfast. That's right—all free of charge! And he would comment, "Just see, we are giving for free, but yet they go to cheaters who charge large amounts of money for some *secret* mantra."

Yoga has become very fashionable as of late, as has meditation and having a guru. Why? Is it that people have a burning desire, a passion, that drives them every day to expand their consciousness and to free themselves from the clutches of maya, or is it because the guru's selling a path that requires little work?

There are no shortcuts to nirvana, my friends.

Anyone who tells you that you don't have to perform some austerity to get there, that you can go out and do whatever you want—drink, have unrestricted sex with whomever the hell you like, and eat all kinds of abominable, violence-produced foods, just as long as you stand on your head and bend like a pretzel while chanting some hodgepodge bullshit mantra, is a fucking cheater. How can a person who him or herself is a servant of the senses, who is bound by the chains of his or her own material illusions, free you?

I've been around the yoga and new age people for thirty-seven-plus years now, and in that time I've seen some of the biggest charlatans on the planet. Charlatans can be found in all the organized religions as well. So many so-called "enlightened ones" have done the most degraded shit. Some of the biggest TV evangelists have proven to be the most materialistic, living in mansions, flying private jets, driving Rolls Royces, having sex with children or whomever they wanted, stashing millions in offshore accounts, and all the while instructing their followers to renounce the things of this world (and give it to them of course), and to live simple, humble lives. Maybe those con artists need to read this: "In the minds of those who are too attached to sense enjoyment and material opulence, and who are bewildered by such things, the resolute determination for devotional service to the Supreme Lord does not take place." (*Bhagavad-gita As It Is*, 2.44)

To exploit and take advantage of people who are at the end of their rope and looking for a way out of hell is the lowest thing you can do. Such exploiters are *sahajiyas*. That's a Sanskrit word that means "Those who take things cheaply." In other words, they tell people they can do whatever they want and still reach some kind of blissed-out state, just as long as they read the *sahajiya's* books, chant his or her expensive mantras, and cough up hard-earned loot so the *sahajiya* can enjoy it.

I recently saw some creepy dude, who was obviously trying to score on yoga chicks, put up a flyer at a local vegan restaurant. It had a picture of him in full lotus, meditating, and wearing all the gear. The poster was advertising his "new" yoga system (seems there's one of those every other day) called "Sahaja Yoga." I said to him, "Dude, do you even know what the fuck *sahaja* means? Turns out he did not. After I schooled him and took his flyer down, handing it back to him, I said, "Your scam needs a rebrand. Go do some research." He looked at me, stunned, then exited.

Let me hip you to some real truth.

Spiritual advancement or any type of work on oneself, be it meditation, yoga, or developing PMA, requires many things of you, but it takes two things in particular: adherence to the system's principles and discipline.

Now, be that as it may, the minute you tell people this, they tell you to fuck off, claiming Swami Such-and-such says I can do whatever the hell I want. Even this book will undoubtedly have readers who will not want to do the work. But there will be others who will let it resonate. They'll continue searching out other, supporting information, will apply its principles, and stay disciplined. Those who do will make leaps and bounds in their personal growth.

And let me reassure you, I didn't come up with what's contained in these pages from my imagination. I simply gathered the knowledge the way a mailman gathers the mail from the post office and then delivers it. Although I've added a few more expletives in my presentation than, say, a fourteenth-century Indian monk would have—but hey, time and circumstance, and that's what the fuck I do. But all jokes aside, in no way, shape, or form do I claim to be any kind of leader, teacher, or guru. I'm just trying to be the best follower of the path I've chosen and to pay forward the gifts I've received by passing on the knowledge to you unchanged. Even if my book helps only one person change his or her life for the better, it's done its job and all my years of research and writing will have paid off.

Know for sure that when we feel deep resistance to some endeavor, it usually indicates a deep need for that particular thing. If you find yourself resisting the work on yourself, don't sweat it. It's natural. We've been conditioned by bad habits for so many years that we can't change overnight. Just keep pushing through. You will hit a clearing eventually. Just don't be the shooting star that makes a big razzle dazzle, then burns out. Instead, be like the moon, constantly effulgent. There will be slip-ups, no doubt, but slipping up and giving up are two completely different things. Remember, we must fail in order to succeed. But don't quit. Quitting things, even little things, will develop in us a quitter's mentality.

I recently had dinner with friend and tattoo artist Chris Garver (Miami Ink). He told me that his mom and dad, both of whom are over 70, went to a meditation seminar in Korea with monks. It was his mother's idea, of course, because his father is your typical old-school skeptic. When his father asked a monk why he should meditate, the monk replied, "Try it for one month and you will see." Well, he did, and guess what? He still meditates to this day.

The monk knew Chris's dad had to dive in and take action if he wanted to experience things in his life, like meditation. The monk knew that once Chris's father took action, he would be hooked.

In the last week I've had over a dozen people hit me up on line and ask if I could give them a meditation exercise. I think the upsurge is because more and more people are looking for a better life and a better state of mind in a world that seems to be spinning toward some real negative shit. It's also due to the medical evidence published lately proving that meditation is good for you. Whatever the case, I think it's great that so many people are starting to wake up and focus on their insides.

A FREE Meditation Exercise— That's Right, FREE!

Now, as for me personally, mostly what I do is mantra meditation. I chant Hare Krishna on *japa* beads. I find chanting engages my mind and senses. My tongue vibrates a sacred sound and my ears hear it. Because I offer and burn incense to help create a spiritual mood, my sense of smell is engaged. My eyes look at a beautiful picture of Krishna while I chant, and my sense of touch is engaged because I'm moving beads through my fingers as I chant each mantra.

The result is that as I chant, my mind fills with beautiful, spiritual images and thoughts. The Bhagavad Gita says that the mind is more difficult to control than the wind. I find chanting Hare Krishna, Hare Krishna, Krishna Krishna, Hare Hare/ Hare Rama,

Hare Rama, Rama Rama, Hare Hare works for me, helping me, as I sit on my meditation cushion, to focus. I also practice controlling my breath, which helps control the mind. Try both as well.

So here's how to do it. Sit on a cushion—or, if you're on a break at work, a chair. Concentrate on your breaths—prana is the energy contained in it. Let negative thoughts and emotions go. Stay in the present. Every time the mind strays, bring it back under the control of the higher self. Remember, *aham brahmasmi:* "I am not the body, not the mind, but an eternal self full of bliss and free from anxiety, stress, and disease." Send healing, pranic energy from your toes to your head and feel your breath become energized. Stay focused on your breath and watch the stress be released.

Do this for five minutes or longer, if you can. Just stay mindful throughout. People have been meditating for millions of years. The great sages, gurus, and philosophers all did it because it works. There was never a day when they didn't have that PMA. You can too if you make meditation part of your daily regimen.

What Do You Mean, Happiness Is a Choice?

Exactly that! Happiness isn't a birthright. Happiness grows over the years through our life experiences, daily practices, and our trials, tribulations, and the realizations that come from all that.

It's the one thing we search for, but unfortunately it eludes most of us. It can't be bought or gotten by collecting more shit. You can't get it from a magic pill, potion, gypsy spell, book, cult, or diet. Finding happiness requires a ton of friggin' hard work.

It's said that the face is the index of the mind. In other words, you can see where people's heads are at because it's written all over their faces. Do a little experiment the next time you're on the subway, bus, or just walking down the street. Study people's faces. Is anyone really happy? Are they smiling? Do you sense they've found inner peace? For nine out of ten people, the answer is NO. Most people are unhappy. You can see it. They're just trying to get through another day. They eat their shitty breakfasts and drag their asses out the door to jobs they hate. They never exercise, meditate, or try to solve their issues. They've accepted *the suck* as reality. The sad fact is, they don't even realize there's another way.

They have no *sadhana,* no practice, and even though they're miserable, many of them ridicule those who maintain their daily devotions or practices as brainwashed. But who's really brainwashed? The ones who are trying to find a better way of life, or the individuals who've bought into the lies on billboards, TV, radio, and the Internet, all of which claim they can make you happy?

And what is that temporary, limited happiness of impermanent sense gratification you're buying into? In Sanskrit, *punah punas charvita-charvanam*—chewing the chewed. It's like taking some sugarcane after it's had all the juice pressed out of it and sucking on the dry pulp. There's no taste left in it that can possibly satisfy you.

The fact of the matter is that human beings are meant for much more than eating, sleeping, mating, and defending. Those things are all that animals do. Humans are afforded the opportunity to expand their consciousness, and when we don't take up that calling, the only possible outcome will be unhappiness, stress, anger, and a never-ending cycle of shitty, bad days.

Now, that's not to say I don't have those kind of days here and there too. Sometimes it strikes, say, in the morning, when maybe I let some rude asshole who almost runs me over on my bike get under my skin, or perhaps a series of events goes down midday where, if I don't catch myself, reflect, and take a deep breath, I would want to choke the living shit out of someone. We have all been in one mental hell or another, but what happens if you don't stomp out those negative vibes as they arise is that they continue rising—and not only in the short-term. It could be days, weeks, months, even years of pent up aggro that can eventually lead to your becoming one unhappy SOB or having a total meltdown, believing the answer can now only be found in your doctor's prescription pad.

The fact is, we all go through peaks and valleys in terms of mood. That's called life. I don't know about you, but I think people who never have an off day are either bat-shit crazy or on five different types of antidepressants. We have to fight through bad moments because they are part of the process. Meds are only a temporary fix to a much deeper problem.

Buddhism teaches that only when we get beyond duality—hot/cold, happy/sad, summer/winter, friend/enemy—do we reach the enlightened state and enter nirvana—or, as the Vedas teach, Vaikuntha, the place free of anxiety. If you want to find lasting happiness, stay focused on your spiritual path and find out who you are.

And just to be clear, I'm not talking about that glazed-over shit I call "hippie-ness" that you get from some whacked dude on mushrooms, Ayahuasca, or LSD. That's still artificial and temporary. I'm talking real-deal, permanent happiness, which, let's be honest, is what we all want. That's the reason we get our tired ass out of bed in the morning in first place—that constant hope that maybe today is the day *it* happens. And then we're beat up by the Enemy Mind in a twelve-round slug fest. Again.

All that can and will change if you work on yourself and follow your process. There will always be stressful situations. What determines your overall mood is how much you let them affect you.

Remember, true character is only revealed under pressure, and the greater the pressure, the greater the revelation.

I've seen many a fake-ass, pseudospiritualist yogi fold like a cheap suit the minute the universe tightened the screws on him. Then it's like, "Namaste, Om brothe—**FUCK YOU, ASSHOLE!**"

Remember, tests are a *must,* and I repeat this constantly throughout this book because we have to realize that tests are part of the journey. So have patience and be forward-looking. All negative energy will pass, but it can snowball into a shit storm if you let it. Don't. Take a deep breath and work through it.

Best-selling author Lori Deschene writes, "You don't have to be positive all the time. It's perfectly okay to feel sad, angry, annoyed, frustrated, scared, or anxious. Having feelings doesn't make you a 'negative person.' It makes you human."

The circles I grew up in on the streets of New York City put me around some pretty crazy and dangerous people. These were the types of dudes who, if they got set off, could easily kill people. As a matter of fact, some did and then paid a heavy price for it. Most of the homeboys I ran the streets with in the mid-seventies and early eighties are either dead, serving life in prison, or strung out on drugs. I didn't want that for myself, so I needed to change.

That started with taking action and watching how I responded to tests when they arose. In other words, I had to take a lot of internal inventory.

The people I'm talking about above are extreme cases, of course, and hopefully most of you aren't capable of that same kind of violence. But hey, you never know. One day you're sitting in rush-hour traffic, an asshole cuts you off and flips you the bird, cursing your firstborn with every four-letter expletive under the sun. You might just get out of the car and go postal. That is, unless you can flip that energy and see that unhappy negative fuckers live for negative drama. As I said, their aim in life is to do harm. They're so twisted in their heads that their happiness (short-lived as it is) comes from ruining someone else's day. Don't be affected by their poison. When you encounter such people, smile and wish them the best as they spew their verbal diarrhea.

And speaking of negative fuckers, remember that old saying "Misery loves company"? Yeah? Good. So keep your distance from them. Those people are like flies, which are always looking for shit. Ever notice how you could be in the middle of the woods, let's say in the forests of northern Sweden (true story) taking a dump—nothing around for miles but acres on acres of trees—then the second that first turd pokes its way out of your ass, the flies are there like stink on shit? Well, some people are exactly like that. The minute some bad crap manifests or people start gossiping about someone else, they rally around and feed the fire. You know what? Fuck those people. Avoid them!

Always look for the positive, and that especially goes for relationships. I've had to cut so many people loose over the years. I just don't have time to waste on the bullshit drama they've created for themselves, especially when I've tried to help them and they refuse to change. Some just have to be left behind for you to stay healthy. As my friend says, "Sometimes you have to 'unfollow' people in real life."

That's why these days I gravitate toward very positive, motivated peeps. That shit's contagious. It's the sure-fire way to get on the road to happiness.

The opposite is also true: negative people will drag you into their hellish world.

Do me a favor and conduct a little test. Monitor those who are never happy. I guarantee you they start off each and every day talking shit about people, posting negative shit on social media, and constantly blaming others for the problems they themselves created. Now, I don't know about you, but if happiness is derived from a set of experiences in everyday life, I don't want to be around individuals who are stuck in their ways and have stank-ass attitudes.

My philosophy is, the moment I open my eyes in the morning I stop, reflect, and see that day as a gift. I've been given another day on earth to do something good with my life. Like my boy said, "Any day above ground is a good day." That's why when I wake up, I immediately offer respects and say mantras (prayers). I acknowledge the new day as a gift. I also take a vow to help someone that day, whether it's to go out and feed the homeless, do something nice for someone, or even just offer a few kind words of encouragement to someone who is struggling. I search out acts of kindness on a daily basis. You have no idea how heavy the statement "Kindness is contagious" truly is.

I find the quickest way to happiness is to go out and try to make others happy. I also make taking action part of my daily positive mindset, my PMA. I make my bed, clean my space, do my sit-ups and pushups, make my juice. I identify the tasks on my corkboard and get to them. You see the process? Action, action, action. I give the mind no time for procrastination (more on that later), no time to wallow in some negative headspace. I beat it into submission. That's my method. You should try that as well. Give thanks when you open your eyes each morning, make your vows to accomplish whatever it is you will accomplish that day, especially in terms of helping others, and take action. I guarantee you'll become a happier person.

I never want to give into the rat race and become some cold, callous fucker. Compassionate people are the real rock stars on this planet, not some D-bag, tattooed, assholes or chicks with bad attitudes that think their shit don't stink. So, words of advice from yours truly, whether you live in New York, London, Sydney, Berlin: be nice boys and girls to everyone you meet. The world doesn't need more bad attitudes. It needs PMA. Life is a gift. Remember that and treat each day as such. You have to work on your mindset daily; it's really what determines your overall happiness. You may not be able to choose what life throws at you, but how you react to it, that, my friends, you have control over.

The best way to beat a case of the blues, or even a depression, is to find positive things that make you feel good and then act on them.

A good feeling will eventually manifest and blossom into happiness. It's a process and one that works. And just to be clear here, I'm not talking about the standing-on the-edge-of-the-roof-ready-to-jump kind of depression. For that, seek professional help.

What I'm referring to here is the kind of depression that manifests over days, weeks, maybe even months. That kind of depression never starts out full-blown; it creeps up on you because you gave into the negativity instead of taking positive action. The solution to this kind of depression isn't more pills, although nowadays, whacko shrinks tell you pills will save you—and they cash larger and larger checks from the pharmaceutical companies (Read: *Confessions of an Rx Drug Pusher*). The real answer is PMA, Positive Mental Attitude, and that comes from taking positive action every single moment of every single day.

The choices you make when you're under pressure prove who you really are. Me, I can't even count the number of times I kicked my endorphins up a notch by going for a good run or working out or riding my bike or going for a swim. Exercise gets rid of my blues, but it didn't cure my depression. Do you know why? Because

I never *get* depressed! I've already been there, done that. I lived on Depression Street for years when I was younger, caused by the seeming hopelessness of my circumstances. Most of those circumstances were beyond my control—but not all of them. Some I had a direct hand in. These days, I stop depression in its early stages. I've been down in them trenches, and I know if I don't nip it in the bud, shit can still get real ugly real fast. I'm not cured of my disease—I'm just telling you that my depression's in remission. And only because I took my meds: my daily dose of PMA.

They say if you don't remember your past, you're doomed to repeat it. I never want to go back to the hell I once found myself in. That's my constant fear, and it's not a bad fear to have. I *should* be scared of that hell. That's why I work each day to avoid it. I don't have to fight the darkness; all I have to do is bring so much light into the room that the darkness dissipates and disappears. It *has* to because it needs to make room for all the happiness. As I said, happiness is derived from a series of experiences, so I want to make damn sure I do everything in my power to make those experiences happen. You do your work too. Fight like hell to become happy. Remember, happiness is not a birthright, it's a workright.

Exercise

Put a piece of blue masking tape across the top of your corkboard. If you still don't have a corkboard, stop reading, get off your ass, and go get one. While you're there, get a pack of 3x5 index cards and some push pins. Next, write

PMA on the left side of the tape. Then, on a dozen index cards, list the things that make you happy. Maybe even add a few of the things I've suggested, like helping others. Pin those twelve cards to the corkboard under PMA.

Then, on the far right side of the tape write **NEGATIVITY**. Take another dozen cards and list the things that put you in a bad mood. Pin those to the corkboard as well, under "Negativity."

Now take a picture of the whole board with your smart phone so you don't forget both sides and watch the events of your day. Which column are you choosing to live under? Your answer will be one of the factors that determine your road to happiness. The simple act of considering the good things in your life will distance you from your own negative thoughts—thoughts that are serving as a barrier to your happiness.

A Word on Grief

Losing a loved one to death or breakup or addiction or some other circumstance can really do a number on you. Sometimes that loved one is yourself, or parts of yourself—such as when your childhood or your adolescence or some part of your integrity has been lost.

Grieving is part of everyone's life because loss is inevitable and nothing else is certain except death. So, of course it's only natural to grieve. But the thing is, you have to push through it. You have to do that for your own survival. You cannot let grief consume your days and nights like some all-devouring fire, or worse, push you to numb your pain by taking drugs or alcohol to cope. During times of grief you really need to apply the methods contained in *The PMA Effect*.

Let me tell you about a man we'll call Steve. I met Steve years ago while feeding the homeless in Tompkins Square Park. He came for months to get food. He never spoke to anyone, but he was appreciative and very polite. I knew this man had a story—all homeless people do. It's so wrong to think they're just bums looking for a handout.

Well, one day it started to rain heavily while we were serving, so Steve helped us rig up a tarp over our table so we didn't have to close down. I took the opportunity to strike up a conversation with him. He told me he camped out under the FDR Drive off the East River. I asked him how he came to be homeless. He paused. I could see the memory was painful for him. I guess because he could sense I wasn't judging him, though, but was genuinely concerned, because he opened up about it. He told me that he had been a hotshot Wall Street broker pulling in a high six figures a year. He had lived with his family—a wife and two daughters—in a doorman building in Battery Park City. His family was his entire world. They took vacations together, the girls attended good schools—basically, this man lived a charmed life.

Then, while he and his family were upstate visiting relatives, his wife and daughters were killed in a horrible automobile accident caused by an idiot drunk driver. And in that moment, his world was destroyed. The grief and pain were unbearable. He took to drinking after work every day and taking sedatives to sleep. Then cocaine got him through the day. Soon he was missing work—first days, then weeks. He spiraled into alcoholism and drug addiction.

Eventually, he gave up hope, then lost his job, apartment, and everything else. He didn't care. Nothing mattered anymore.

Steve closed himself off from the world. He stopped talking to his family members and friends and lived by collecting bottles on the street and cashing them in for a little food. He also went to food distribution programs around Manhattan. When it was warm he lived in a cardboard box on the FDR, and when it got too cold he went into the subway stations. This had been going on for three years.

I was stunned to hear his story. I couldn't begin to imagine what he must have been through—the amount of suffering involved with his particular type of loss. We talked a few more times when he came by, and when he asked, I also told him some of my story. Then he stopped coming. Months went by. I hoped he was okay. I asked other homeless people who knew him from the FDR encampment, but no one had seen him.

Then one day out of the blue he showed up again to help us serve. Steve was clean, sober, and wearing nice clothes. He said he had come out in order to pay forward what he had received. He had never forgotten what we'd done for him. He said he had been so lonely back then, and the hot meals we were serving along with the little bit of conversation he'd had with me was enough to get him through another day.

I asked how he'd overcome his grief. He told me that one night, he found himself standing on the Manhattan Bridge, ready to jump. That was his defining moment. He thought of his wife and kids.

When they were alive, they would do anything to make him happy. He saw their faces in his mind's eye—and they were sad that he was about to take his own life. He broke down crying. Then he stepped off the bridge and vowed never to touch drugs and alcohol again. He moved into a shelter, found a job, and dug himself out of the hole his grief had created in his life. Imagine the internal strength that took. His true character was revealed. He was indeed a warrior.

Unfortunately, the sad truth is that a lot of people in his shoes would have jumped. I've seen so many I've known over the years commit suicide. For them, something happened and they couldn't shake off the grief. Grief spirals into serious depression and can grip you like a champion grappler if you let it. I have family members who self-medicate because of past traumas. Shit, I used to do it too. When I was on my two-year crack, pill, and booze tear, I even wished one of the drug dealers I was robbing would just end my misery with a bullet.

But in the end I reached out and begged for help.

If you're grieving, you must reach out. Don't go it alone. People *will* help.

I know some of you reading this now are suffering loss. Remember, one stick is easily snapped, but a bundle of sticks is much harder to break. So seek out good association. People have compassion; most of them will know what you're going through because no one has made it very far in life without suffering. Grieving is part of life, but when it turns into a very negative situation, you need to reach out. Suicide is not the answer. It only leaves a trail of destruction behind.

Fight like a warrior and get shit off your chest. There are people who will listen, but you have to be honest about what you're going through. My friend from Tompkins Square Park to this day attends NA and AA meetings, talking to others who may be where he was during that dark period of his life. He's paying it forward.

MRI for the Soul

When was the last time you actually sat back and monitored your internal life, your feelings, emotions, happiness?

Have you taken inventory lately on where your spiritual practice is at? Those who remain constantly mindful answer that they take this type of inventory almost daily; others say they never do it at all.

> **If we're caught up in the rat race, we can easily lose sight of what's important in life.**

Now, I'm not suggesting you ignore your daily needs for making money to support yourself; rather, I'm suggesting you dedicate as much time, if not more, to your internal quest.

The material body is made of earth, water, fire, air, and ether. The subtle body is made up of the mind, intelligence, and ego. Who are you? Are you that gross or subtle material body? If you were, you wouldn't say things like "my hand," "my mind," "my intelligence," "my body." Who is the "my"? Who owns your body and mind?

These are deep questions, and if you consider them you'll find that you are none of those gross and subtle bits of matter but the self inside them, a passenger, the person who knows the body and mind and their field of activities.

It takes self-reflection around these matters—self-reflection is mandatory in developing a deeper and truer sense of self. Getting to the know the self allows us to think of more eternal goals and happiness. If you fill your life only with what's temporary, you'll end up only with things that are temporary, fleeting, impermanent. Remember, we come into this world empty-handed, and we sure as hell leave empty-handed. There are no luggage racks on top of that hearse, my friends.

One of the many books I read daily to help me focus on what's important, what's internal and eternal, is India's classic, the Bhagavad Gita. Although there are many Gitas out there, I read *Bhagavad-Gita As It Is,* by A. C. Bhaktivedanta Swami Prabhupada. The Gita teaches about the soul and how it is completely transcendental to the body and mind and therefore beyond the limitations of matter. It teaches us to identify with something truer about ourselves—the platform of self where we can tap into our unlimited potential. If we remain fixed in this spiritual consciousness even when we're under pressure in this world—which we certainly will be—then we'll find ourselves having the resilience and strength of self to deal with them.

These days—really, in every era—there's much pressure to fit in and be accepted. This pressure especially affects younger people—I mean, look at all the bullying that goes on. Some of it has, unfortunately, even led some kids to commit suicide. The solution to peer pressure is spiritual grounding. If you know you are beyond the temporary body and mind, then there's no need to convince others of your self-worth; your self-worth is rooted in the truth about yourself, so it gives you confidence and perspective on how to pursue your goals with integrity.

> **Social status actually doesn't matter. You don't need to make it into the right clique of so-called cool people or some scene. Think of all the bullshit that goes along with that.**

We all want our lives to matter. Most of us want to make a positive contribution to society. In order to do that, we have to look inward and get past all the superficial crap this materialistic society tells us to strive for. Those are distractions.

When symptoms of illness appear in the body, those systems are a warning that something's not right and we'd better go for tests to find out what's happening. We might be sent for an MRI. Well, the symptoms people are exhibiting these days—depression, drug addiction, overeating, drinking, anxiety, and worse—tell anyone watching with any awareness that the soul is ill. How do we diagnose and heal the problem? Simple. Reflect, look inward, do things that contribute to your internal life. Read, study, and then apply what you've learned. Take a break from mass media, commercials that are trying to sell you shit, the club scene, and the Internet.

The Bhagavad-Gita 9.2 states, "This knowledge [of the self and what you capable of doing with your life] is the king of education, the most secret of all secrets. It is the purest knowledge, and because it gives direct perception of the self by realization, it is the perfection of religion. It is everlasting, and it is joyfully performed."

And the purport that follows, by Srila Prabhupada, states, "Generally, people are not educated in this confidential knowledge; they are educated in external knowledge. As far as ordinary education is concerned, people are involved with so many departments: politics, sociology, physics, chemistry, mathematics, astronomy, engineering, etc. There are so many departments of knowledge all over the world and many huge universities, but there is, unfortunately, no university or educational institution where the science of the spirit soul is instructed. Yet the soul is the most important part of the body; without the presence of the soul, the body has no value. Still, people are placing great stress on the bodily necessities of life, not caring for the vital soul."

Rest assured, he's talking about something that's beyond religion, which isn't always focused on the self or soul. That's why the

Gita calls the knowledge it's teaching "the *perfection* of religion." Knowledge of the soul is what serious religionists are striving for. In an attempt to speak to everyone, even though all religions have similar soul-based teachings, churches and temples and mosques often stick to a dogmatic or blind faith, and some even get lost in fanaticism, none of which can bring you closer to truth.

In closing, I hope I've left you with something to think about. Hopefully, you'll at least walk away from this section with questions for which you can then seek answers. The willingness to inquire about the nature of life is a sign of real intelligence. I remember when I first got into philosophy, yoga, and metaphysics, I'd sit around for hours with my friends discussing things of substance. It was an amazing experience and it really opened me up. I think that kind of inquiry is missing from today's youth culture. There are so many distractions. It's the same for us older peeps, too. I mean, have you checked out the shit your friends post every day online? 99.99 percent of it is complete and utter bullshit nonsense. That's why we need an internal, spiritual MRI. Taking that kind of inventory is the first big step in implementing PMA and finding lasting happiness.

PART THREE

Removing Stumbling Blocks

If you're trying to light a fire, don't throw water on it. This section of the book will address things that will crush your daily PMA and set you back on the path. If you become aware of those negative traps, you'll know what to watch out for.

Don't Play the Victim— the Blame Game

I can't stand it when people makes excuses for being fuck-ups because they had it rough. "But John, you don't understand. I'm a drug addicted, two-bit, lying, cheating, scumbag thief because my mother never gave me enough hugs, and sometimes at school I opened my Spider-Man lunchbox and discovered that she'd forgotten to put jelly on my peanut butter sandwich!"

Seriously, get over it and grow the fuck up. That's exactly what I had to do it in my life because my "real" friends had the balls to tell me the deal instead of enabling me to continue in my self-pity. Some of the most accomplished people on planet earth had to overcome some of the most difficult circumstances to get where they are.

Playing the victim ultimately means we can sidestep our own shortcomings while we focus on our suffering and the faults of others. And that means we don't have to fix *our* shit.

I mean, God forbid we turn the focus on ourselves.

Now that I stopped playing the victim card and blaming others I am able to use my past as incentive to motivate me to get somewhere and to never give up and go back to that former life. So rather than bitching, moaning, and blaming, wanting everyone to feel sorry for me, I made a conscious choice to fight day by day to change the path I was on. The first thing I did was get sober. I knew I had sobriety in my control, that it was up to me. You do too. Fix things right away. Just do something to get started on that. For me, it began with exercising and maintaining a clean, plant-based diet. I meditated and started a yoga routine. I took what was in my immediate power and started there. When you follow that process, you'll find out what you're made of.

The fact is, if you think everyone will treat you right in life, you're setting yourself up for a letdown. I'm fully aware there are jerk-offs out there, both male and female, so when somebody acts the fool and is disrespectful, it shouldn't flip me out. I've met some very advanced souls too, people who actually accepted the mistreatment they got from others as their own karma. One of my good friends never gets rattled when others do him grimy. He simply accepts it and says, "It's God's grace to push me forward on the path." That's an advanced state of consciousness, and by no means am I there. But I can strive to get there, as can you.

Playing the victim card allows us to avoid responsibility for our lives, for our mistakes, for our happiness. We can just go on making excuses, blaming others for bad shit we may have, in fact, created. I'm speaking as an adult of course—not as a child who may have bad situations forced upon him or her. There are also those who play the victim card to justify their abuse of others. I know some of these people personally, and I avoid them like the plague. They're toxic as hell. Although they can flip the script on their lives and create healthier circumstances, they don't seize the opportunity because they want to play the victim role just so they can mistreat other people.

Life will always give us shit to complain about. Things are always going happen, someone is definitely going to do you wrong, situations will not turn out the way you'd hoped. But playing the victim doesn't get you anywhere. All it does is make you point the blame elsewhere. You don't have to fix anything because, hey, it's not your fault. This attitude is very dangerous; it will stunt your emotional growth. Make sure when bad things arise in your life that instead of playing the victim, you take responsibility and work your ass off to fix or heal whatever problems or obstacles have appeared on your path.

Be Mindful of Criticizing Others

"Criticism is the only reliable form of autobiography."

— *Oscar Wilde*

Now, to be clear: I'm not talking about constructive criticism—the kind that comes from a positive place and is meant to help someone. I'm referring here to the destructive type.

Always be mindful of how your words may impact others.

Personally, I'm pretty thick-skinned, but not everyone is. Some people don't deal with criticism at all. So always be compassionate. You may destroy someone's self-esteem with ill-chosen words—so much so that in extreme cases, he or she may shut down or, even worse, harm him or herself.

Some people don't think twice—or, as they say, have no filter—when it comes to criticizing others. In reality, though, when people spread poison, it's usually because of feelings they're having or things they're trying to deal with in themselves. They're actually broadcasting to the world what they themselves need to fix. My advice is before you say anything, always consider whether you need to say it at all. Then make sure it's coming from a good place.

Never Procrastinate, Waste Time, or Give In to Resistance

Look at how much time can be wasted when you procrastinate. You could waste weeks, months, even years, letting them slip by as you slip further from your goals.

Time truly is our most valuable commodity. Ancient Indian politician and philosopher Chanakya Pandit once said, "Time is so valuable that if you pay millions of gold coins, you cannot get back even a moment." That's exactly what procrastination does: it squanders your valuable time. You miss opportunities, then lament about what could have been, if only. Procrastination can seep into any area of your life, from your career to your relationships to taking care of your health. The more you put things off, the more work they'll seem to be and the more pressure you'll feel. All that will mess with your self-esteem: "Why doesn't anything happen for me? WTF is wrong with me?"

I see these type of self-sabotaging posts every day on social media. I monitor that shit for some of the people who come to me for advice before I step in and say something—not from a bad place but as constructive criticism. Then it's up to the people I'm talking to to listen and not waste time on nonsense, procrastinating while they could be doing something of real substance. Procrastination can and will destroy your self-confidence over time. Then rather than PMA, you'll end up with something on the opposite end of the spectrum, a shitty attitude.

> **That's why your word is so important. When you say you're going to do something, by God, make it your business to get it done. You must be impeccable with your word.**

Not following through on things will definitely destroy your reputation on some many levels with so many people. Even on the streets it's said, "All I got is my word. My word is my bond." Putting things off constantly only makes matters worse, especially when it comes to caring for your health. Let's face it, an unhealthy body or mind can ruin your life. Procrastination is a deep form of resistance.

I've mentioned Steven Pressfield's book *The War of Art* here and there in these pages. In his book Pressfield talks about giving in to resistance: "Resistance is experienced as fear; the degree of fear equates to the strength of Resistance. Therefore the more fear we feel about a specific enterprise, the more certain we can be that that enterprise is important to us and to the growth of our soul. That's why we feel so much Resistance. If it meant nothing to us, there'd be no Resistance."

And what can be more important than flipping the script of your mental life from negative to positive? Believe me, it's a lifelong battle but one well worth fighting. By entering this battlefield, you'll create a whole new journey for yourself, and that's why resistance will attack the hell out of you.

The first step in fixing any problem is to recognize there is one. As many sage people say, deal with fire, debt, and disease immediately. Well, procrastination is a type of disease. Some people spend their entire lives worrying about the future instead of dealing with the present, with the problems and desires and opportunities right in front of them in the here and now. Procrastination is a way to avoid working with those things, which in reality are the only ones over which we have even a little control. No one knows what the future holds, but when it arrives it'll still be the present, and if you're a procrastinator, you'll push that future date away just as easily as you push away today's.

Every day we can fight miniwars that lead to victory in the overall battle on the war against resistance. Giving in, quitting even small things you said you'd do leads to bigger problems. For one, you develop a flaker's mentality. If you say you're going to wake up early and jog three miles, get your ass out of bed and do it by any means necessary.

You have to do things especially when you don't want to. A deep resistance to a particular task usually indicates a deep need for it—those tasks are usually related to self-improvement. As you try to change for the better, expect resistance. You'll find yourself saying, "Ah, you know what? I'll start that yoga next week." Don't. Start it today. And procrastination breeds negativity because it creates a sense of unrest as you avoid things, leaving the unconscious mind in a constant state of agitation. You should know that things you want to do but then avoid never quite make it off your unconscious to-do list.

You know what you have to do, so stop putting it off. The water may be cold, but once you're in, you'll get used to it—it'll actually feel good. No different with tackling tasks. The Enemy Mind will make even the littlest, easiest thing into some huge issue. That's why we need to constantly beat it with a stick. That can only be done, as I mentioned earlier, by engaging the mind under the direction of the intelligence.

I love the analogy of trying to light a fire while throwing water on it at the same time. On that note, let's look at one of the main reasons many people can't get their asses into gear, why they procrastinate, and if they do take action, don't give it their all.

OK, You Party Animals

If you want a sure-fire way to fuck your life up and get nothing done, do drugs and drink. Now, I'm not talking about an occasional glass of wine or a beer with friends; I'm talking about taking these substances into body and mind day after day. It's no coincidence that most people who do that are also the biggest slackers when it comes to matters of any substance.

I have a friend here in NYC, and he called every meeting about his business plans "networking." Now, did these so-called networking meetings happen at his apartment or in an office at 6 a.m.? Hell, no! They involved going to clubs and bars to have drinks. Drinks led to cocaine—you know, just to keep all that business talk flowing. Then, after this productive night of networking, my friend would top off the evening with Zanax, Valium, or whatever the hell else he had to take just to get to sleep at 4 a.m., once the bars closed.

Would you like to know what business he's in now? Bullshitting and scamming people. He even managed to hustle his own mother, draining her life savings so he could continue his full-time job of being a drug addict.

As for me, I'm sober. I avoid even that champagne toast on New Year's Eve because I'm an addict and always will be. I choose not to get high or to drink today. My disease is in remission. I'm fully aware just how easy it is to start down the slippery slope back toward addiction. Taking those substances into my body would be like playing Russian roulette. Besides, I love the feeling of staying clean and sober. It feels great. Sobriety is good for my body, mind, soul, and especially my PMA.

Drinking or any drug use can wreak havoc in your life. You probably ain't gonna go do that run, bike, or work out at the gym if you got fucked up the night before. And if you do, by some strange miracle, your performance will be total shit.

Another one of the many books I've read on my journey is *The Science of Self-Realization*, by A. C. Bhaktivedanta Swami Prabhupada. In it he says that intoxication destroys austerity. Austerity? It means undertaking hardship to achieve a particular result. By that definition, one of the many austerities I've embarked on is trying to fix the *fucked-up* me. It's been a battle, and I'll be the first to admit I've had some serious issues and still have some. But by keeping my wits about me and staying sober, I'm able to stay in the fight.

Speaking from personal experience, some of the biggest flakes and depressed people I know (I'm not referring to clinical depression) are people who get fucked up all the time. Whether it's in pursuit of their careers in music, acting, training, writing, or LIG (life in general), they talk the talk but never walk the walk. See, resistance loves people who get slammed all the time because then it has a drinking buddy. Your drinking buddy will tell you, "It's okay, John, have another. Everything's gonna be alright." But as Steven Pressfield said, "Resistance is always lying and always full of shit. It will con, cheat, and fuck you over."

Please don't make the mistake of thinking that I'm faultfinding here. What I'm doing is pointing out the pitfalls that can crush your effort and spiral your life out of control.

Remember, addiction never starts out full-blown; it creeps up on you.

The fact is, since I got completely sober I've worked hard, shown up every day, stayed motivated, kicked ass on my projects, and am never depressed. Even if I get a case of the blues, by the time I've gone for my run, swim, ride, done my meditation, or gone to the gym, the blues are gone. You can only give up a lower taste by replacing it with something higher. Trying to be artificially happy by getting stoned or drunk will get you nowhere. In the long run, it actually takes you further from your goals.

Also, let's take a look at the root of the word—in-**TOXIC**-ation. Get it? You're poisoning yourself. I don't need booze, weed, pills,

MDMA, or Ayahuasca to have a good experience. I'm on a natural high. Things that affect your mind actually bring you down off the higher vibration of your natural spiritual nature. Don't let people peddle that bullshit to you with some hallucinogenic. Remember what it is—a drug. You're not experiencing a blissful permanent spiritual moment when you take it; you're having a temporary drug episode. When the drug wears off—poof, the experience is gone.

I know people who had so much going for them but pissed it away by taking intoxication. I'm not here to preach but to suggest what worked for me. That said, I've only accomplished what I have thus far because I no longer get drunk or party. EVER. Matter of fact, I was up at 5:00 a.m. this morning to train for my upcoming Ironman. After that, I went to the Lab to write. Try doing either the training or the writing with a hangover or while you're crashing from MDMA ingestion. So here's a mantra to remember: **Intoxication Destroys Motivation**.

Test yourself

Try full sobriety for one month and watch how everything falls into place. Your relationships with others will improve, you'll eat better, have a desire to exercise, and you won't flake on your projects. You'll wake up in a good mood and maintain it throughout the day. Getting fucked up can never solve problems; it can only mask them temporarily.

What's with All the Complaining?

Do you know why happy, successful people don't complain much? Because they're too busy figuring out ways to turn negative situations into positive ones.

Simply put, they don't want to invest energy in things that won't achieve success or change things that need changing. No one is going to deal with a complainer for too long, either. Me, I listen, then offer advice. If the complainer doesn't take it, I step off. There are only so many hours in a day, and I just don't have time for complainers or ask-holes (who ask for advice but don't follow it).

If things aren't happening in your life, rather than bellyaching constantly, seek out ways to fix it.

You might want to go back to the "Procrastination" section above and take a look at how much time you allocate to the pursuit of your dreams and how much you waste on bullshit. If I claim to be a writer but only spend an hour a day writing and four hours on Facebook or watching TV, am I really trying to be a writer? I don't think so.

Now, don't get me wrong. I vent plenty. It's good to blow off steam, but there's a big difference between venting and being a chronic complainer. Chronic complainers always have drama; something's always wrong. Somebody always did them dirty at work, in their relationships, their bands—and their shit is always more important than everyone else's. I mean God forbid *you're* having an off day, because I can assure you they don't want to hear about it. They're too consumed by their own narcissism.

News flash: there are a lot of people—in fact everyone you meet—who are dealing with things, but most of them don't broadcast it to the world on social media. Seriously. I've been deleting a ton of those fuckers as of late. But you know who's comments I hit the "like" button to? People who roll with that PMA.

One of my friends, whom I knew had cancer and had just gone through a divorce, never complained. Well, he beat the disease, has a wonderful new relationship, and his career has taken off.

Do you think that would have happened if he was busy playing the victim, procrastinating, or complaining all the time? I bet that woman he's come to love and his employer were attracted to his energy, because he was the epitome of a Positive Mental Attitude.

Try and focus on the good things in your life. If there aren't any, make some. You have that power. *The PMA Effect* is all about self-empowerment. If there's a problem with someone, work out a way to solve it. Confront the person, but tactfully. Often when someone is spewing his gripes to me about someone else, I say, "Joe, did you tell *X* this?" Nine times out of ten the answer is no.

Constant complaining does nothing to fix issues. What it will do, though, is push your people away and spin you down into lonely, dark mental hells.

You will give into the Enemy Mind and may later find yourself on some barstool drinking shots with some negative fucker.

I will leave you with these wise words from author Eckhart Tolle: "To complain is always nonacceptance of what is. It invariably carries an unconscious negative charge. When you complain, you make yourself into a victim. When you speak out, you are in power. So change the situation by taking action or by speaking out if necessary or possible; leave the situation or accept it. All else is madness."

Stop Stressing

Stress is a killer. It's been medically proven that too much stress triggers bad things in the body. Stress also affects your thoughts and behavior.

Left unchecked, stress can contribute to a number of health problems, including high blood pressure, heart disease, obesity, diabetes, and more. Stress also affects the neuroendocrine system, causing high levels of cortisol to be released, which affects your adrenal glands, causing fatigue or failure.

We all have to deal with stress, but each of us does it differently. Some of us work through it while it drives others to fly off the handle. I know I've reacted to stress like that in the past. I'm not above anger, but I'd like to share some exercises I now use to deal with stress. The main one is to stay mindful. Perspective. Previously, when someone pushed my buttons or something happened in my day that wasn't pleasant, I'd react harshly. Ironically, the by-product of the stress and my reaction to it was more stress. So these days I try to take a step back, reflect on and analyze the situation, and see it as a test meant to push me foward in my self-improvement. I'm not always successful in controlling my stress, but hey, I made the effort. As long as I keep trying, the desired result will eventually manifest.

That said, being able to monitor and manage stress starts with being able to recognize its symptoms. How does your body respond to it? When you're in a dangerous, stressful situation, most people's flight-or-fight response is activated. Your heart rate and blood pressure rise, your palms get sweaty, and adrenaline is released into your bloodstream.

Have you ever seen a corner man in a fight tell his fighter, "Okay, now, deep breaths." One of the top MMA trainers on the planet, Greg Jackson, does that all the time. In the middle of all that chaos, all that stress, he tells his fighter to meditate and control his breathing. It's not just to increase his oxygen intake; it's to help his fighter deal with the stress of battle and to stay mindful and centered. In that state, the fighter is able to reflect on his months of training. He focuses all his attention on Greg's instructions, but more importantly, he's able to apply them when the buzzer sounds for the next round.

So remain mindful when you're facing a stressful situation. Watch your thoughts, emotions, and how you're responding to them.

How you respond to stress will tell you a lot about yourself. It's worth studying. It will also show you what tools you have or need to develop in your arsenal. Do you know why the military puts their Special Operations recruits under the most stressful conditions imaginable? It's to teach them to rely on countless hours of training in order to push through any obstacle. Cool heads always prevail, especially in war (or the war of life). If you can't keep cool under stress, if you lose your shit, you're gone. That's how the military's Special Ops selection process works. They push you to make decision after decision under intense, relentless pressure.

So what I tell myself and others when they're flipping out—is "Yo, take some deep breaths. Just breathe. It'll pass." Deep breathing is calming. That's why in yoga, students learn to control the breath. A controlled, calm breath is essential for meditation. I use deep breathing techniques all the time. It's very powerful. Your breath is full of prana/energy. Anger pollutes the body and breath, shutting down the third-eye chakra. When you practice your breath-relaxation techniques (I'll give you some below), your heart rate slows, blood pressure stabilizes, muscles relax, and blood flows to your brain, which means your overall energy and focus increase. I'm telling you, I've done this deep breathing during some of the hardest moments while racing Ironman, and it works. Your ability to solve problems increases tenfold.

A positive mindset, PMA, is your most powerful weapon against stress. It's stronger than any drug, prescription or otherwise.

I've seen people make some very bad choices when they're under stress, especially when that stress has led to them to anger. If you sit back and monitor your stress, you'll see there's a pattern to your responses. Stress can creep in, grab hold, then choke the living shit out of you. Don't let it happen. This book is about trying new ways of doing things. Instead of smacking that rude person next to you, try the following tips to help manage your stress. Some of them might even look familiar by this point in the book.

Practice, Practice, Practice

Set aside time. Schedule times to practice. I find it's easier to practice your breathing, meditation, or any other self-time practices first thing in the morning when you're fresh and before your day gets in your way. I also take time in the middle of the day. And don't bullshit—you have five minutes for it. What you invest is what you'll get out.

Don't expect perfection out the box. Expect ups and downs. You aren't going to have major breakthroughs every day. That's just not realistic. You'll have them, though, guaranteed—as long as you make the investment in your practice. You may even miss days. Don't be discouraged. Shit happens. Remember, slipping up and giving up are two different things. Start again and push through.

Be mindful during exercise and meditation. I see at the gym that instead of focusing, many people stare at the TVs mounted above or on their exercise machines. Stop it. Please. My trainer's gym has NO efffen TVs. He wants you to focus 100 percent on movement and breathing, on how your body feels. Even while meditating, the mind can carry you away, focusing on your stressors instead of your practice. Stay mindful!

Breath is Life

- Sit comfortably in a quiet place (no gadgets) with your back straight. Focus all your energy.
- Breathe in through your nose and exhale through your mouth. Watch your breaths. Note your mood.
- After each breath cycle, you'll feel your stress diminish. Listen to your body. Now go to that happy place.

Don't Eat Shit Food

Again with the friggin' food, John? Yeah, and I'm harping on this point because I know how important diet is in our overall physical and mental health. So diet is a natural follow up to the stress section because what you eat so much affects your mood. Bad diet can also make the body stressed, and acidic, which leads to disease. Not to mention how stressed out you're going to be when you're running to doctors and hospitals all the time and shelling out big bucks for all those drugs they have you on.

The power of plant-based foods comes from their abundant vital nutrients—nutrients your body needs to fight off stress. Foods like spinach, kale, and other greens, fruits and nuts, beans and legumes, veggies, whole grains, chia, quinoa, and other seeds, are nature's antidepressants. I can speak personally on the power of what a good, organic, whole-food, plant-based diet has done for me in terms of my mood. The first catalyst pulling me out of my hell was changing the way I thought about food. Something clicked inside my crazy, fucked-up head, and my whole consciousness changed. That was the first step ultimately leading to me changing my life.

Now, maybe you're telling yourself that eating a pint of ice cream or a burger and fries helps you deal with stress. It's comfort food, right? Let me ask you, What's so *comfortable* about hemorrhoids, quadruple bypasses, the pain of diabetes, or having part of your cancerous, rotten colon ripped from your ass and having to crap in a colostomy bag? Want a wake-up call? In *Meat is for Pussies* I break the science down for you about what meat and all that processed crap does to the human body after years of ingesting it.

On the flip side, think about all the stress the animals you're eating have been under for their entire lives and right up to the moment of slaughter. Like humans, stressed animals release toxic stress hormones into their bloodstreams, which invariably enter their muscle tissue. I don't know about you, but I sure as fuck don't want to eat that. And we don't have to. The science is out now about the abundant benefits a plant-based diet offers you in every area of your life. There are also incredible foods out there waiting to be discovered. So answer the phone; the future's calling.

But even when you're eating healthy foods, you can still obsess and stress. I see those types all the time. I call them macropsychotics. They all look bat-shit crazy and unhealthy, too, despite the good food they're eating. Every little food issue causes them to obsess, stress out, and melt down. "You fucking oversteamed my broccoli, asshole!" So you need balance even in terms of diet. Eat to live, don't live to eat.

Did you know I had an eating disorder? Not the throwing-up type—shit, the state didn't raise no fool: I wasn't wasting all that expensive organic food! I was an overeater. I think I developed this one because I was starved as a kid. As an adult, I always had an unconscious fear that food would disappear again and I'd go hungry. Now, couple that with a shitty, depressive relationship, a back injury that prevented me from training, and you have a recipe for disaster. I ate until I was ready to explode, and then I ate some more. Food became my drug, my coping mechanism. I ballooned to nearly two hundred pounds. Want proof? Go watch that CBGB's DVD with the Cro-Mags. I had more rolls than a fucking bakery back then.

The point I'm making is that when you start on a positive road, you won't want your physical vehicle breaking down on you. Caring about what goes into the body is a must if you want to achieve a positive mindset. But don't obsess like a macropsychotic, who actually loses sleep and needs therapy and meds if, God forbid, he or she eats a fucking french fry. There's a happy medium. Find it and stay balanced.

So eat healthy if you want to avoid trouble down the road. And let's be honest, a lot of obese people eat for emotional reasons. They're hurting inside just like I was, and like me, many of them medicate with food. Well, one way to reverse all of that and change is to start a healthy lifestyle and eating regimen. And, of course, follow what's in the rest of this book.

There are also what I call unconscious eaters. For that, let's back up a second and go back to the section on getting wasted. Some people stuff their faces with complete garbage when they're fucked up at 4 in the morning and leaving a club. Why do you think those cocksuckers with the schism cancer carts cooking shish-ka-bobs made of mystery meat and grilled horse dicks are stationed out front? They know you'll pony up to them for some of those Weapons of Mass Destruction because your decision-making process has been compromised. If you saw that crap in the light of day, most of you would vomit.

Anyway, are you starting to see how all of this ties together—the partying, the food, the bad attitude, the stress—how it's like a puzzle with all the pieces fitting together? You don't get to pick and choose. That's the deal we made at the beginning of this journey.

You have to follow the *entire* PMA process, and that includes the dietary stuff.

I can tell you from experience that there will be a major shift in your consciousness if you do. Positive vibes will fill your life, and positive vibes attract positive people. Remember, this is coming from one angry, fucked-up, drug-addicted criminal. I mean, shit, if it worked for someone as damaged as me, it can work for you or anyone.

Try This:

Eat a whole-food, plant-based diet for one month. Meditate. Practice mindfulness when you're stressed. Avoid negative people. Get plenty of rest. Stay drug, alcohol and tobacco-free. Exercise daily to get your endorphins flowing. Breathe! If you don't feel better in thirty days, I'll buy the damn book back from you.

Don't Identify with Negative Thoughts

I struggled big time with negativity. Negative thoughts entered my mind and I'd dwell on them for hours, letting them consume me. They'd fester like a cancer.

Sometimes I'd be in a bad mood for days. I got migraines. Dwelling on negativity rather than working my way through it and finding positive solutions to my problems has been one of my stumbling blocks over the years. I had so much pent anger and aggro toward people who did shit to me as a kid. When I gave time to those negative thoughts and let them take hold, it put me in the worst mood. I'd lash out—sometimes even physically. It took me years of work on myself to overcome this, and I still struggle with it from time to time.

The first step in my healing process was to stop identifying with the thoughts, to see myself as aloof from the mind and its ever-flowing poisonous crap. Negative thoughts ebb and flow like the tide. So stay mindful.

The more you practice awareness of your thought patterns and what they're doing to you, the faster you'll redirect your energy to something positive.

The ability to redirect is like muscle-building. If you want to develop your muscles and become strong, you have to exercise daily.

I do my mental exercises because of this. I practice seeing myself as separate from my mind and thoughts. If negative thoughts enter the mind—and trust me, they do—I take a step back, then immediately refocus my mind on something positive. Someone talked shit about me? Big deal. I'm going on a bike ride, and in an hour I'll be out at the beach, soaking up Vitamin D from the sun and practicing PMA. Then when I get back, I'm going out to feed the homeless. When we learn to see ourself as different—as above the mind— we identify with the essence. We are spiritual by nature. Know that. We say "My mind," not "I mind." See? Remove yourself from the mental platform to your higher self.

Don't give negative thoughts room to turn into negative emotions or, worse, bad actions. Anyone who has known me for a long time knows that I hemmed up many a chump in my earlier years for talking smack. Now, that smack-talking rolls off me like water on a duck's back. I just don't give a shit. Their words reflect *their* negative world and can't touch me as long as I don't identify with the negativity. I can't; I've got too much positive work to do.

The other thing I've noticed in my fifty-five plus years on planet earth is that we often blow things out of proportion. We let that seed of negative thoughts take root. We even water it with our words and actions. But when we take a step back and deal with things objectively—when we take our emotions out of the equation and base everything on fact—we'll usually discover quickly that whatever it is is not a big deal.

Develop your inner strength and you'll choose to change destructive thinking to constructive thinking. Getting drawn into negative thinking all the time is like building a prison for the mind. If you want to be free, pay attention to your thoughts, how they compound, and where they lead.

Our thoughts play a major role in our lives and health.

For example, when things don't go your way, do you immediately tell yourself you're not good enough? We can criticize ourselves constantly, you know. We all know people who do that, who are extremely hard on themselves. They focus on their flaws instead of what's good in themselves and their lives.

So learn to let things go. As souls conditioned by self-ignorance to one degree or another, we're flawed. The Vedas categorize those flaws into four basic defects, true of anyone who's living a conditioned life: (1) we each make mistakes; 2. we each have the tendency to cheat ourselves and others; 3. we each operate under so many illusions; 4. we each have imperfect senses. So we're all works in progress striving to become better human beings. That won't happen overnight. But if you put in the work, if you show up every day, eventually you'll get where you want to be. So let them negative thoughts go. As Bob Marley said, "You just can't live that negative way. You know what I mean. Make way for the positive day."

Let Them Grudges Go

Most of us are guilty of this at some point. I can tell you that a grudge is one hell of a heavy burden to carry around. To err is human—we all make mistakes. We do, and others do. So learn to let things go.

I'm not telling you that to forgive means you have to become friends with the people who did you grimy. I'm just saying that your life and attitude will be better when you can forgive and move on.

Forgive, but don't forget. I'm clearly not suggesting that by forgiving you then let someone continue to walk on you. There are those out there who will. I've had to forgive certain people for doing some vile shit to me, and I've let some of them back into my space, thinking perhaps there was a way to fix things and rekindle old friendships. That's just sentimental most of the time. Yeah, I got swept up in the old reminiscing-about-the-good-old-days bullshit, you know, back when it was "real," hoping there was a way to relive it. One person used this to his advantage and, with his premeditated plan tried to fuck me over again. Lesson learned. Remember, a leopard can never change its spots.

That's why these days I'm pretty short on patience. I have to be, because I have no time for drama. I'm too focused on getting my tasks done. If someone knowingly does something to fuck me, I cut that person out of my life. Out of sight out, of my mind. I hold no grudges or ill will; I just move on. Sometimes shit happens and arguments arise, but two healthy adults will usually resolve their differences in positive ways. But the ones who live to harm, the envious, who show their true colors time and again, well, they get their walking papers.

Hating someone and carrying a grudge is like carrying around a heavy toxic load on your back.

It will eventually consume you and make you sick from the stress and anxiety of it. It may even cause serious depression if the betrayal was by someone you were close to. Let it go. If the friendship or relationship was real and the other party truly valued it, he or she will sincerely apologize. Then it's up to you to be big enough to accept it and, depending on the circumstances and the relationship, continue on or release that person.

So keep your life free of ill will and grudges. Keep your mind focused on the good in your life. We've already discussed the working of the Enemy Mind. Well, that Enemy Mind will look for anything negative and throw you for a loop. Grudges especially. Your day can be going great, filled with positive endeavors, you're working on your projects and getting your shit done, and then— there's a reminder of *that* person or persons. The next thing you know, you're spiraling down into a world of negativity. Been there, done that. I imagine we all have.

So the more you can practice forgiveness and let those grudges go, the farther you can walk down the path of PMA without getting sidetracked on your way to your goals. Your relationships will also be happier, and your day-to-day dealings with others more pleasant. You have no control over the way people treat you. That's on them. What's in your control, though, is how you respond to it.

Don't Hang Around With Negative, Unproductive People

They say you can tell someone's nature by the company he or she keeps. Well, right the fuck on to whoever came up with that one, because I couldn't agree more.

You want to be negative, complain, bitch, moan, get wasted, play the victim, take things personally, quit everything you do, and never get anywhere in life? Then hang out with those who do that shit for a living.

Their mental diseases are contagious, though, so look out! As they say, fools go undetected until they open their mouths. When what comes out is useless verbal diarrhea, especially when that's coupled with a culture of wasting their days and nights getting high, run for the hills, my friends, and never look back.

It's no coincidence that people who get fucked up all the time are constantly at the top of this list. I know people with huge amounts of talent but who started the negative snowball rolling by getting high, creating an avalanche of negative shit that consumed their lives.

If you want PMA, you have to hang out with those who practice PMA every day and avoid the others. That's what I do; I surround myself with happy, successful people, driven people—those who exude PMA. I learn from their experiences. I've been down that other road for far too long. I'm over it. I suggest you get over it too.

These above-mentioned unproductive people are expert at pointing out faults in others. This is because they have too much time to waste. Instead of using their time to look at their own lives, they put everyone else's life under the microscope. They try to mask their insecurities and failures by trash-talking others.

Don't get involved in that drama. Use all of your time productively. Make shit happen in your life. Think about all the time that can be spent doing unproductive, time-wasting things that will get you nowhere, then flip the script and use that same time for your projects.

Minute by minute, hour by hour, day by day, do the work. If you can do this, I guarantee things will happen for you. You'll become truly productive, someone who accomplishes what you've set out to do, someone who understands fully that time is your most important commodity and that you can never buy back even a second of it for all the money in the world. When you approach

DON'T HANG AROUND WITH NEGATIVE, UNPRODUCTIVE PEOPLE 221

every day with that mood, who has time to hang around negative people?

There's a reason people get together in one group or another, join one slice of society over another. It's to help each other stay fired up, to inspire, to find strength in numbers. That's true even on the spiritual journey. In Sanskrit that's called *sanga.* It refers to association with those who choose to operate from a higher vibration, who are devoted to the spiritual path. That's my go-to crowd as of late—the ones who walk the walk and who operate from the most positive places and get their shit done under any and all circumstances. I need these types around me. I'm honored and privileged to be able to learn from them. I hope some of their good qualities will rub off on me. And the others—the members of the crumb-bum society—I avoid them like the plague. You should too!

Dating or Marrying the Wrong Person

I know what you're thinking—relationship advice from John Joseph? But hear me out, because I've been around the block a few times and have learned some valuable lessons in the relationship department.

Dating, or worse, marrying someone who is completely wrong for you, will put you in a world of shit. Relationships take a hell of a lot of work, and you're going to spend all your *me* time with that person. So if you want to be happy in life, why the hell waste time with someone who's completely wrong for you?

I've made this mistake more than a few times. I got complacent and comfortable and saw no reason to break off the relationship, even though my significant other caused me strife every single damn day. There would be times I wouldn't even want to go home because I had to deal with her. This was when I hurt my back, couldn't exercise, was overeating and blowing my body into obesity. I was the most miserable person. I was getting high from the painkillers they were giving me for my back—but getting high to numb the emotional pain along with the physical.

I know many of you can relate—you've been there or are there now. We constantly pick a person who's wrong for us because we're afraid to be alone. We go from relationship to relationship, problem scenario to problem scenario, sometimes wasting years. You're doing no one any good by living a lie, so stop trying to push that boulder up a hill. If you waste time with someone who's wrong for you, then you are not leaving an opening for the right person who may be out there. Besides, if you find that the work of being with someone is in constant conflict with the work you must do on yourself, it's a clear sign that the relationship is unhealthy.

Relationships must *never* take precedence over your self-work. Do you hear me? You come first. That's not selfish; I'm giving you real talk.

Being in a relationship will never make the man or woman. No one else can fix us. We have to do the work on ourselves and make things happen. If you meet the right person, he or she will be the cherry on top. And who is that right person? It's someone with whom you can work to grow as people.

My woman has told me many times that she's glad she never met the old John Joseph. I know what she means. I was a fuck-up.

It took me years of hard work to make myself someone I'd want to date. I had to do a lot of soul-searching, and I spent years alone while I did that. I was alone, but somehow I wasn't lonely. Do you know why? Well, first off I had my Enemy Mind to keep me company, and second, once I beat that fucker into submission, I had time to think about who I was. If you don't search for meaning in your life, you'll always feel lonely whether you're alone or in a relationship. Without a strong sense of self, there'll always be a void no relationship can fill.

So make yourself whole, and then, in time, someone who has a parallel path will manifest. We attract the energy we put out into the world. Remember that. And if you're in a bad spot in your relationship or marriage, try your best to work it out. But if there's no workable solution, even after counseling, and you guys are at each others' throats, and you've done everything possible to honor the commitment you made to the relationship, especially if there are kids involved, step off. Just make sure you remain civilized. I know in some cases the anger left over from the relationship can make that hard, but for the sake of your children and for your own sake—and even for the sake of your significant other—you have to rise to the challenge of it. Don't hold grudges.

There are exceptions, of course, to keeping any ongoing relationship civil, such as in cases of domestic violence. If you're suffering from that, do what my mother did to my a-hole father and tell the guy to go to hell. If he doesn't listen, get help.

Oh, and divorce is not a free pass for you to become a deadbeat dad or an absentee mom. Your kids don't deserve to be punished just because you guys couldn't get along. I have friends who got divorced and both parents remained in their kids' lives. Kids need two parents, their mom *and* their dad, so remember that and do whatever it takes to keep the PMA between you two. Then when your kids are grown they will respect and thank you for taking the high road.

Envy is Whack, So Stop Hating

"Do not overrate what you have received nor envy others. He who envies others does not obtain peace of mind."

—*Buddha*

It was definitely an envious person who wrote the book on how to make enemies and piss people off.

Envy is the real root of all evil. Some of the most miserable people I know are also the most envious. They spread their poison when anyone around them accomplishes anything—some even go out of their way to do so. Cut those people out of your life like a cancer.

Be mindful of any envy in your mind and heart and be happy for others' successes. Revel in the happiness of others.

You know that more than likely, those people found success by sacrificing and working their asses off. Knowing that about them inspires me; it shows me that if I push, I can get there too. So why should I be a hater? Haters have some serious self-doubt issues going on.

I heard a lot of people say that you know who your friends are when you're down and out. *Bullshit!* Let's see who has your back and is happy for you when you're kicking ass and great things are happening for you. Those are your true friends. I've seen that when good things started to happen for many of my friends, their so-called friend camps shrunk. That's because they were surrounded by envious, snakelike people. All it took for envy to manifest in those "friends" was for their friends to become successful. It's like giving milk to a serpent—the milk of happiness others have achieved only increases the venom of those who envy them.

In misery and failure you'll have legions of friends who console or compare, but climb out of that pit and watch what happens. Success is a catalyst for your friends to polarize. You'll see quickly who in your friend camp is full of shit. You'll quickly find the snakes, those who were laying in wait to bite when the first good thing came your way.

So do this exercise: even if you don't particularly like someone, try to be happy when something good happens to him or her. Then sit back and watch what happens to your attitude—how it changes for the better—and with that infusion of PMA, you in your turn will be able to accomplish more. I even wish success for those who wish me ill. Ahimsa: never wish harm on others. That's not my job. Everyone gets the karma they deserve, so if some shit is coming to them it will come regardless of what I think. I don't need to pollute my consciousness by wishing ill will or failure on others. I know one miserable fucker who tried to cast spells on people, as if he was some powerful yogi or magician. Guess what?

All the bad shit he wished on others backfired and his own life went to complete shit.

On the surface, this issue of envy may seem like a small thing, but once you peel back its layers and realize how deep it goes in yourself, you realize it's the one negative emotion at the core of almost all human suffering, especially for those digging mental ditches for themselves.

If we can eradicate our envy we'll be much happier people on the whole. Our relations with others will improve. Our country and planet will also improve. The more people who get clear of their tendency to envy the better the planet will be. Doing this, of course, takes a universal consciousness, where we can see all other creatures as essentially no different from ourselves. But how can we see them like that when our envy makes us covet their possessions or accomplishments? That's really why we put down the achievements and characters of others—we think their achievements and qualities should be ours. Paramahamsa Yogananda quoted his guru on this point in his amazing book, *The Autobiography of a Yogi:* "Some people try to be tall by cutting off the heads of others."

Got it?

Hating doesn't make you tall; it makes you a very small person.

So be happy for others and you will always remain happy. Flip the energy wasted on envy to PMA and get your shit done. Nobody likes the petty mentality of an envious hater, so don't be one. Instead, be a well-wisher to all.

The Four Disagreements

I want to mention again a book that's helped me tremendously to stay on course with all my passion projects. It's called *The Four Agreements,* by Don Miguel Ruiz, a Toltec shaman spiritualist.

After reading his book I realized I was guilty of breaking every single one of the Four Agreements. Now that I was aware of it, I couldn't stay stuck on stupid. See, that's what knowledge does: it makes us realize there's a problem, then offers a formula so you can solve it. It's science, really. You apply a formula and get a result. To the degree that you apply the formula properly and without alteration, to that degree you get the desired result.

The Four Agreements are: 1. be impeccable with your word; 2. always do your best; 3. don't make assumptions; 4. don't take things personally. Simple, right? Yeah, but put those into practice every day. I found I didn't express how I felt about situations to people who'd wronged me, so I'd bullshitted and told them "It's all good." Not anymore. Now I get shit off my chest. As politely as possible, of course.

Once I'd read *The Four Agreements* I discovered that for most of my life I'd been practicing the Four *Disagreements.* I had a shitload of work to do, I realized, because many of my problems stemmed from the fact that I had things ass-backwards. I'm willing to bet some of you do too. **If you find you're doing the polar opposite of the Four Agreements, reevaluate and fix things.** Let's have a look at the Agreements in a little more detail.

1. **Be impeccable with your word. Speak with integrity. Say only what you mean. Avoid using words to speak against yourself or to gossip. Use the power of your word in the direction of truth and love.**

You have to constantly be on guard with this one. Trash-talking can easily sneak up on you and ruin your day. In the Vedas it says that of the five senses, the tongue is the most difficult and voracious to control. The tongue wants to taste things, yes, but even more it wants to wag. It's so true! Monitor your words carefully throughout your day. When you find yourself gossiping or smack-talking, bring the tongue back under the control of the intelligence. My intelligence has told me that from experience, if I talk smack I'll feel like crap later, so instead I try to engage in dialogues of a positive nature. Or I just don't talk. I quiet the mind and spend some time on reflection.

Social media is filled with too much talking. Some people seem to think that what they say online doesn't count. They're sadly mistaken. I know in the past when I've engaged in negative, destructive words, it brought nothing good to me. Now I concentrate on speaking encouraging words, spreading PMA, and trying to help others. I let all the other toxic words go, and that's let me feel much more positive and productive.

Being impeccable with your word also means doing what you say you'll do. If I give my word to someone else or even make a pact with myself, I have to follow through. Only an act of nature can stop me. I've learned that every time you break a promise, it chips away at your integrity. Remember, little flakings lead to bigger ones. Don't minimize the importance of your integrity—your word. Being impeccable with your word, especially in terms of speaking the truth, will change your life for the better.

> **2. Don't make assumptions. Find the courage to ask questions and express what you really want. Communicate with others as clearly as you can to avoid misunderstandings, sadness, and drama—just this one agreement can completely transform your life.**

I can't even tell you the number of times I've created false scenarios in my head and run with them, landing in a world of shit.

I've let myself think I knew what some other person was thinking or planning—that he or she was plotting against me—only to find out I was way off. Keep the channels of communication open. Don't let things fester. Deal with things that are bothering you straight on. You know what they say, "When you assume, you make an ass out of you and me."

This one agreement can solve so many of the world's problems. Always remember that each of us comes from a totally different set of experiences. Misunderstandings or even just different perspectives are inevitable. So keep the lines of communication open. Nine times out of ten, the people who have negative conflict and drama in their lives have broken this Agreement.

3. **Always do your best. Your best is going to change from moment to moment; it will be different when you're healthy than when you're sick. Under any circumstances, simply do your best and you will avoid self-judgment, self-abuse, and regret.**

When you always put your best foot forward, even if there's a bad result, you'll know in your heart of hearts that you gave it your all. You'll also know that you'll aim to do better next time. People who slack off never have peace of mind. They're always agitated and pointing out others' faults.

Let me draw a comparison between two people I know in this regard. This first person has degrees in engineering, business, and finance. He even has a license to buy and sell real estate and another to buy and sell stocks. A resumé of the careers he's had in the last decade would fill two pages. Every six months he creates a new life master plan and then he's off to something else. He has genius IQ, but he never rises to the top of anything he does, never finishes projects. He has so much God-given ability and smarts, yet he always seems to fail. Why do you think that is? I'll tell you. Because he's a slacker. He's taken all that ability for granted. This person is always looking for a shortcut, a hustler's way out, so he doesn't have to do the work. He sleeps until noon and goes out at night to network over drinks. He falls into this cycle of changing careers and again hustling his way through repeatedly, and he has become an unhappy person.

There's another person I know who doesn't have such a high IQ and has no diplomas hanging on his wall. But every time this person does anything, he gives it his all. He's 100 percent invested in what he does. Never slacks. He's up before dawn every day tackling a new adventure. He finishes projects. Even if there's a discrepancy in his work, he willingly goes back to fix it. He doesn't drink, smoke, or get high because he wants his mind clear to focus on his goals. He makes sacrifices. This person has been happy every time I've seen him. He never has a bad word to say about anyone, but rather, is always encouraging, listening to other people and sincerely wanting to know what they're up to and whether he can help in any way.

So who do you think will get further in life? You already know the answer because you know these people—we all do.

After reading don Miguel's book I went to see him speak in New York City. Actually, someone gave me tickets as a birthday present. It was one of the best gifts I've ever received, and being there was life-changing for me. Don Miguel elaborated on this Agreement during his talk, and it was right at a time when I needed to hear it, because things weren't going my way with my writing career, fitness, head space, or relationships.

I realized after listening to him that the reason for my slowness was that I wasn't all in. I was half-stepping, always holding back from being completely invested in what I was doing. As soon as I changed my mentality, the light came on. Things happened. I finished one book, then another. I wrote scripts, got an agent, got in shape, have since done multiple Ironman triathlons, and gotten the right girl. Now sure, none of that happened overnight, but he inspired me to keep trying and remain invested, to always do my best. You have to make sure that whatever you do in life—no matter how seemingly mundane that thing may seem on the surface—you have to do it with heart and soul. Be all in, completely invested. And that attitude will carry over into every aspect of your life.

4. Don't take things personally. Nothing others do is because of you. What others say and do is a projection of their own dreams. When you're

immune to the opinions and actions of others, you won't be a victim of needless suffering.

This last Agreement can save you much aggravation and grief. It's also probably the most difficult to practice. That's because when people do grimy things to us or speak bad about us, we want to lash out at them, sometimes physically, but often with our words—breaking the first Agreement.

Don't. Instead, understand that a poisonous, toxic person living in his or her own hell will never speak kind words or perform kind acts toward you or anyone. Matter of fact, I'll bet the farm that they have beef and drama with dozens more people besides you. And sometimes the people lashing out don't live in hell all the time. These people might be our friends or significant others, and they may be lashing out in a moment of pain. It might even have been triggered by something we said. Still, their lashing out feels like a betrayal especially because your relationship with them is so good. Still, you should understand that it has nothing to do with you—it comes from their own pain.

Hands down, this is very hard to apply, but its also the most rewarding. Ever since I began to see painful words or deeds in this way, I've been more able to let things go, and that made me happier. I walked with PMA. One very advanced friend of mine told me to say a prayer for the people who constantly talk trash or try to bring me harm. Truth is, they need the prayers. Stay bulletproof, poison-proof. Actually, to see that trash-talking comes from others' pain is a compassionate perspective. It only becomes your truth, though, if you accept it and act accordingly.

Here I'd like to add a **Fifth Agreement** for the readers of my book: *agree* to get *The Four Agreements*. Read it; apply it. Following those agreements is the only way things meant to bring about PMA and change for the better will work. Remember, it's not about how far we may have come but how far we have to go. The ability to grow, the numbers of experiences, and the amount of knowledge are unlimited. So is your divine human potential. Keep learning and do everything in your power to become a seeker of truth.

PART FOUR
Your Go-to Actions

It's vitally important to always remain focused and to set goals. To achieve those goals requires tons of hard work, dedication, and mindfulness, especially if you set a high bar for yourself, which, of course, you must. If you remember to work with PMA along the way, huge boulders blocking your way become pebbles you can simply kick from your path.

First Things First

When you wake up in the morning, set your mind on the positive frequency and think of the victories you'll have over the course of your day and on all you'll accomplish.

Do *not* lie there, roll over, hit snooze, and scratch what needs scratching. Scratch it on the way to your corkboard. Look at all your tasks for the day and plan to take action.

Doubts, bad thoughts, and resistance tend to take root especially in the morning, so as soon as you open your eyes, say your prayers or whatever you do to express gratitude, jump out of bed, shower, make a juice, and get at it. Don't lay around contemplating ... what if? Instead, take action. All the Enemy Mind needs is a single loophole, the slightest of crack in your warrior armor, and your morning will be a wreck along with the rest of your day. Don't let the Enemy Mind get that toe-hold. Beat that sucker down with a stick. As the badass Marines say, "*Carpe diem*—seize the day!"

There Is No App For This

I recently saw a segment on CBS 60 Minutes about mindfulness. Top CEOs who get big things done went to a meditation retreat run by this cat named Jon Kabat-Zinn.

Jon's been practicing meditation and teaching it for forty-seven years. He started doing it as a way to help people cure their medical conditions. Yeah, a positive mindset can do that.

Well, the first thing he did was make reporter Anderson Cooper and the rest give up their electronic devices—no cell phones, iPods, laptops, TVs, or radios in their rooms. Even alarm clocks weren't allowed. No distractions whatsoever. The retreatants were just to *be present* in the moment.

So they quieted their minds and watched their thoughts. Each time the mind went off, they brought it back under control. They practiced eating in the moment, walking in the moment, even showering in the moment. They also had amazing discussions.

These days when I go out to eat I watch how people interact. Many barely talk—just tap, tap, tap on their little devices. They never even look at one another or what they're eating. Human interaction is decreasing with the rise of technology. Even when walking down the street people don't look at one another. They've become texting zombies, commenting on posts on Facebook, Instagram, or Twitter as if what they're writing is of biblical importance.

As a native New Yorker who was raised on the streets, I find it imperative to look around. I have to look people in the eyes. That was once a survival tactic for me. Now I just love human interaction. Not to mention that you have to watch your back, because there are still some crazy-ass, dangerous people walking these streets. Needless to say, tech zombies are easy prey for them.

Anyway, the rewards the people at Kabat-Zinn's retreat attained were so amazing that they went back to their companies and had their employees do ten minutes of mindful meditation a day. Google was one of those companies; they now start employee meetings with a hundred people in an auditorium meditating and being in the moment. Do you know what's happened at those companies? Productivity has skyrocketed. The benefits of mindfulness can affect every aspect of your life—your career, your social experiences, your spiritual life, and your physical and emotional health.

So when was the last time you meditated for even a few minutes? Meditation is vitally important.

I gave you an exercise to help you extract yourself from the rat race, and I'm going to repeat myself here: wake up and quiet the mind. Spend time being silent, reflective, in the moment. Take inventory of your thoughts and slow down the relentless flow of bullshit. Go outside and walk down the street and pay attention to everything—your breath, your thoughts, the people, the birds scrambling for crumbs. Watch every one of your steps. We take so much in life for granted.

The other day I saw a young man with cerebral palsy using a walker. The struggle he endured just to make it down the block was incredible. Yet he was smiling while many people with healthy bodies were grumpy as hell. I actually took a moment then and thanked God for that opportunity to appreciate what I too had taken for granted.

If you're working on developing a positive mental attitude, how the hell do you expect to do that if you let life's moments pass you by while you're caught up in gadgetland, constantly texting, checking email, your Facebook status, your stocks, posting photos on Instagram. It can wait. It can *all* wait. Unplug, people! Experience life. Have conversations. Dig people's vibes. That's not hippie shit but happy shit. That's PMA in action.

Start by allocating time in the morning to mindfulness. No gadgets. None. Zip. Zero. Zilch. Get up and sit silently in a room you didn't sleep in. Have a meditation area in your home. Sit and take inventory. Focus on your goals. You can even try it at 2 in the afternoon, when the stress of the day is starting to get to you.

Rather than having a meltdown, turn inward. It's been proven that people who meditate for even a few minutes a day have a better mental attitude, are more productive, and the real kicker? They're happier.

A trait common to unhappy people is loneliness. Sometimes it stems from a lack of social interaction—many are so addicted to social media that they forget to talk to anyone in real life. This is a sickening trend these days, especially with young people in the U.S. and everywhere else in the world. Adults are guilty of it too, and it's no wonder that as a species we're becoming some of the most miserable fuckers to ever walk the earth.

Some people are completely distracted by the constant bombardment their gadgets offer them from the moment they open their eyes in the morning until their heads touch the pillow at night. They walk around devoid of any real contact with others and missing any genuine contact with their own bodies, minds, and emotions. And holy shit, if I even say hello to one of these people on the street, they go into total shock mode. "It does not compute! Danger! Danger! Run, Will Smith!" He panics as if I'm putting a gun to his head and about to murder his ass.

See, me, I come from an age before all this technology. I'm not saying technology doesn't have its advantages, but it shouldn't control every waking moment, making us shells of ourselves. Reducing interactions between humans limits our growth. We need one another.

I enjoy meeting people and conversing. I've become much more mindful these days. I never take things for granted and never, EVER, walk down the street while texting. I try to absorb every experience life has to offer and realize what gifts those experiences are. I know I'm at least on the path, and no doubt it's hard work to stay there, but one of the by-products of my path—I'm pretty fucking happy. You can be too.

Yo—Zip It!

There's nothing worse then a flapper—meaning, someone who's constantly flapping his gums but never getling his ass into gear.

Flappers tell you about all the amazing things they have going on, then a week later you find them making excuses for why their so-called "master plan" never manifested. The funny thing is, with all the social media available, people bragging about all the things they're going to do has hit the point of the ridiculous. When you search their stuff a week later, it's like, "Yo, big mouth, where'd you go?"

This "talking" gum disease infects flappers even during important times, such as when someone is trying to educate or instruct them on how to move forward. They never hear what their instructors say because their minds are either thinking about how to respond or they're already talking—trying to show their abundant knowledge. In the end, they stay stuck on "stupid."

So the first step in getting moving—and in receiving any type of knowledge— is to open your ears and hear.

In Sanskrit, hearing is called *shravana*. You hear, then you remember (*smarana*). If you get those two down, you can then try to apply yourself to the endeavor. Even in traditional martial arts you have to bow humbly before your Sensei and ask to be instructed. You don't walk into a dojo and talk shit, as if you're the all-knowing, demigodlike badass. That all-knowing shit is called "false ego," and you can be sure the Sensei will make an example out of you very quickly. Even my Great Irish Aunt Betty Burke always said, in her deep, gravely, smoker's voice, "You got two ears and one mouth, so zip it and listen twice as much as you talk."

I'm not really a book guy. I mean, sure I read, but not like the kind of people who read a dozen books a month. Most of what I've gained I've received through a personal connection with a teacher. The teacher talked; I listened. That was my process for learning to retain knowledge. Had I been talking, I wouldn't have heard what the teacher had to say. I've also discovered over the years that the best teachers are also the best listeners. They have to be, because they lead by example. They too had to hear from their teacher, their guru, their Sensei, and then apply the knowledge. When they did, they became qualified to instruct others. This holds true in any teacher-student scenario. Every type of teacher in every field—from spiritual gurus to master martial artists to great writers to athletes to Spec Ops warriors has had to listen to a teacher, remember what was taught, and apply the lessons.

Hear submissively and then be a doer, not just a talker. Follow through on commitments and projects no matter how big or small they are. Once you start the process of becoming a student who listens, remembers, and acts, that energy will carry over into all aspects of your life. It's part of maintaining PMA. Never stop pushing ahead and never stop hearing.

Listen carefully to your teachers. Hearing properly is actually a science. If you sit ten people down with a speaker and then ask each what he or she heard, I guarantee you there will be ten different answers. Even this book—you're hearing what's written here, right? Rest assured, my dumb ass didn't come up with all this info. I simply heard properly for years from the many amazing teachers I've met, and now, as part of my action plan, I'm sharing it with you.

Take notes. Memory is tricky. I write things down. Even in business meetings I ask if the other participants mind if I take notes. Why? Because I don't want there to be discrepancies between what I heard and later what people say was said.

I cannot drive home enough the value of proper hearing. It's vitally important. Start by quieting your mind and shutting your mouth. Proof of your good hearing is your ability to apply what you learned—when you turn instruction into action. Try it. I guarantee that this method will help you get your shit done and raise the level of your performance. Pay attention to who gets things done and who flakes. Most of the top-tier achievers are expert listeners.

Although it may seem deceptively simple on the surface, the hearing process is actually deep. I've noticed a direct correlation between those who get their tasks done and their ability to pay attention to the detail through what they learned through proper hearing. The opposite is also true: those who tend not to finish tasks seem to always be talking when the teacher is talking, as if they know a better way—their way, of course. Later, they complain about how life sucks and blah, blah, fucking blah. The fact is, if they'd zipped their lips and heard properly, then followed through from there, things would change for them.

I have many friends who are much more accomplished than me in many areas. I would love for some of what they got to rub off on me. So do you know what I do? Inquire submissively from them and shut the fuck up. The devil is in the details, so I pay attention to detail. Again, that's why they drill listening and attention to detail into your head in the military. What if you're sent into combat? With life and limb on the line, you're dealing with the highest level of value and risk. They know full well that it's human nature to choose the path of least resistance. That's never the right path, though, when it really matters.

If everything you do is easy because you took the path of least resistance, then you need to question how high you set the bar and how difficult your challenges are.

I guarantee that if you look at that, you'll realize you've set it too low and have seriously underestimated your potential and ability.

Risk and the Level of Reward

Those who never risk anything and prefer the path of least resistance will live lives with little meaning, quiet lives of desperation.

Not me. I always want to push the envelope—become self-realized, do yet another Ironman, write more books, movies, TV shows, feed all the homeless people in NYC, and other shit, and I want to do it all by 6:00 tonight.

I know that's not possible, but you get my point. Do you know what the thing is about my goals, dreams, and desires? They all began with me be willing to take a risk. Many great opportunities have come my way because I was willing to risk something. Even if I failed at some of the things I've risked, I've learned valuable lessons. And those lessons allowed me to try harder or try differently the next time. Taking risks builds confidence and courage. As I said earlier, opportunities knock, but you still have to kick that door down. And not knowing what's on the others side—ah, there in lies the risk.

But taking risks should never be done half-ass. You have to be serious and apply yourself 100 percent all of the time. When I went to take a scuba lesson, one of the first things the instructor said was "Pay very close attention to everything I'm telling you. Take notes. You can die doing this." There's that *hearing* thing again. See, if we're going to step out and risk in a big way, expecting big rewards, we need to hear properly. Risk is a great teacher. You need to be a great student.

If self-esteem is the bright side of risk, fear and failure are the dark, shadowy side.

That's why people create buffers between themselves and their families and anything that might be dangerous. Bubblewrapped in a tidy world—I see that a lot with parents these days. They don't even want their kids to go out and get a few bumps and bruises in any pursuit, or to punch a bully who needs punching. Rather, they want to protect their kids from the kind of life experience that might toughen them up a bit and teach them to reach for the fruit hanging higher up the tree. Kids need a thick skin to survive life, and that's exactly what risk gives them. I'm in no way suggesting I'm an expert on parenting, but I know what worked for me as a kid. Kids don't have to face the kinds of dangers I faced in order to take risks; they have to come up against adversity, though, and be presented intellectually or physically or artistically or in some other way with more than they think they can actually do. A little pressure helps a kid step out of the world of easy kudos, of sixth place trophies, and into a world of actually working to develop themselves, where they're molded into go-getters. It all starts with stepping out of one's comfort zone and taking a risk. True for kids; true for adults.

The fact is, the world is a risky place with unpredictable plot twists no matter how many buffers we may try and put in place and things will always come up despite our best efforts. So my advice is to be fearless, go out, risk more, and, again, fear less. Embracing risk will ultimately help you overcome fear of failure in other aspects of your life. You have my money-back guarantee on that.

Gratitude = Attitude

Let me ask you something: as you go about your daily routine of work, kids, training, school, or whatever, do you take time to stop and give thanks for your life's gifts?

The beautiful array of colors at a sunrise or sunset, the smell of fragrant flowers, the smile of a stranger, kind words from a friend—all gifts. If you answered "Not lately," or worse, "Never," please pay close attention.

The problem I have with our culture's obsession with social media, nonsense gossip, TV talk shows, and them whack-ass reality shows is that they draw us even further from the internal and the important, leaving us wallowing in the shallow, the mundane. In that state we lose sight of what really matters in our short time on earth, such as telling people we care about them, being kind, helping others, and always remembering the principle of gratitude.

When we overcomplicate our minds by filling them with so much inferior bullshit, and plug our energy and beings into a system that dictates that we must live only in a certain way, a way that leaves no room for self-realization, our hearts can easily harden. We become, in fact, nothing more than polished animals simply eating, sleeping, mating, and defending.

And, oh, how we love to defend in every way possible—from our personal, day-to-day conflicts, where we argue like cats and dogs, to nations like the U.S., which have made huge leaps and bounds in making war a big business. Actually, war is now the norm in America, but any combat warrior will tell you that war is a societal ill, not a virtue. Only wannabe Rambos, who've never seen a day of combat, glorify it.

Yes, we work hard as hell for a little sense gratification at the end of the day, and we've developed distractions galore to help us ignore that haunting question lurking in the back of the mind: Why am I here? Now the alarm has gone off to wake us from sleep.

Waking is the first step in the process. Then, like children, we have to spend every day soaking up knowledge.

Look at the awe in the face of a young child encountering something new—the gratitude and appreciation they have for it. It's really a wonderful quality and unfortunately one we tend to lose as we grow older and more conditoned—when we become those *serious* adults.

My life changed dramatically when I started to inject the principle of gratitude into my daily practice, when I saw everything as a gift and gave thanks for it. My whole attitude shifted. We plant seeds and then harvest the seeds we sow. I'm the farmer who every day plants seeds of PMA. When I was new to meditation, one of the first things I was taught was to slow down, breathe, relax, take inventory, think of all the good in my life, appreciate it—essentially to stop taking people and things for granted and develop gratitude. I found when I felt gratitude first thing in the morning that I was able to walk around in a positive mood all day. I had that PMA. We have so much in America and the Western world, yet we continuously focus on what we don't have, yet that just leads to hankering, overconsumption, and ultimately, anxiety.

I went to Jamaica in January 2015. I didn't stay at one of the all-inclusive resorts locked away from the locals. I went out and experienced the island's culture. Soaked up the knowledge of the Rasta medicine men—their science of roots and herbs, healing fruits and vegetables. Many people on the island live way below what we in the States would consider the poverty line, but they always seem to be smiling and happy. And they're grateful for even the smallest of gestures from their visitors.

So be grateful for everything, even the bad stuff.

In my memoir, *The Evolution of a Cro-Magnon,* I even thanked my asshole, scumbag father for being a dickhead, and I meant it.

I did it because I had to recognize that how he treated me made me who I am today. Even the foster father who beat my ass and starved us I now thank. Tests, even traumas, are there for a reason. Be thankful for those and do what you can to grow from them.

It's said that gratitude is the healthiest of all human emotions. The more of it you express, the more likely you will find even more to be grateful for. This is an important principle for those interested in attaining PMA. People take so much for granted—a healthy body, the air we breathe, the water we drink, the food we eat even as we unconsciously stuff it in our face. But sit back before you chow down the next time and take a moment to think about the abundant variety of fruits, vegetables, seeds, nuts, grains, the colors and fragrances of the herbs and spices—and all of it coming from dirt! I'm not pushing God on anyone, but I thank Krishna every time I eat, and before I eat I offer my food back to Him, because I'm grateful to be able to eat food that can heal my body and give me energy. And to the scientists who claim it's all molecules, I say, okay, start with nothing, start from scratch, and make me even one grain of basmati rice.

Remember to have gratitude for every area of your life. Be thankful for friendships, a great meal, or the fact that you're healthy enough to run, bike, exercise, or work at anything at all. Practice an attitude of gratitude. Always remain in the consciousness that nothing is owed to you. The entitled can never be happy. I've seen that one personally—people who rely on their past laurels as if because they had a hit record or movie twenty-five years ago, the world should kiss their asses.

Don't fall into that trap. Be grateful for every day your eyes open and you are given more time on this planet. When you develop that type of gratitude, you won't waste time—time will be valuable to you. Stick firmly to this principle; develop an attitude of gratitude and watch how quickly positive things manifest in every aspect of your life.

They Ain't just Words

"Watch your thoughts; they become words. Watch your words; they become actions. Watch your actions; they become habit Watch your habits; they become character. Watch your character; it becomes your destiny."

—*Lao Tzu*

I mentioned this in the last section, but now I will elaborate on it because PMA is a process and words can poison the process if you're not careful.

The tongue *is* the most voracious and difficult to control. It wants to talk shit, eat shit, and cause shit.

The thing is, you can never really recall your words. Be very careful, then, diligent, about what you say.

Think before you speak. What are the likely repercussions of my words? Am I about to give the best possible answer? Did I consider all the options before I dispensed advice? Am I motivated by kindness by what I'm about to say?

Out of every possible thing don Miguel could have written in his book, he chose to tell us to be "impeccable" with our word. Don Miguel knew that a big factor in the direction your life takes—and the lives of others take—is affected by which words you choose to speak. Your words shape minutes, hours, days, weeks, months, and years of your life and the lives of others. Give serious consideration before you let them manifest in the air. Think about the butterfly effect and how you're not exempt. Try not to say things you'll regret.

You do have the choice to use your words to encourage and heal others. Doing that will find you taking huge strides in your PMA. When you speak, you plant seeds of beautiful fruits and flowers or weeds. So think twice—hell, think *three* times—before you speak. If the pen is mightier than the sword, use the power of your words to do good, to help others, to never to put others down. Remember, what comes around goes around.

I have to say that in my own experience, taking the advice of friend and bandmate A. J. (Leeway/Cro-Mags) on this changed the energy in my life. He told me never to speak ill of others—even those who did me grimy. It was hard advice to follow, but gradually I did it. I put his instruction into action and created an aura of positive energy around me. Then positive people were drawn to me, and along with them came positive things. All possible because I redirected wasted energy on negative words to getting my shit done.

These days, I do what my friend does when someone is talking trash about somebody else—try to change the topic. If that doesn't work, I walk away. Gossip is almost always an expression of envy. The minute I let go of all that small-time gossip and shit-talking, the moment I chose a different road in life, everything changed for the better. Including my circle of friends.

I've stayed friends with people who are growing. Those who choose stagnation and dwelling in the negative I had to leave behind along with their highway to hell. Many still talk shit and spread poisonous lies and gossip, but we don't have to listen to that anymore. Let your days and nights be consumed with speaking positive words and trying to make positive things happen in your life as well as in the lives of others. And you know what? It works! I'm on my third book, and the other two I wrote have helped a lot of people. Watching my words worked!

Confidence Is the Cat

I recently saw an incredible video on the internet. An alligator had turned up in some people's backyard, and as they were filming the seven-foot monster stepping out of the water behind their home, their small cat appeared out of nowhere.

The cat's hackles were raised and it looked ready to strike. It's attitude caused the massive beast with jaws of death to stop in its tracks. The cat stared down the alligator blocking its path, confident, sure of itself, ready to protect its territory at any cost, and not seeming to consider that the alligator outweighed it by hundreds of pounds and it could snap it up in half a second. The alligator even opened its mouth and showed its teeth, as if to say, "Hey, buddy, you see these?" But the cat was not shaken one fucking iota.

Actually, I thought, as did the people filming, that the encounter was going to end badly for the cat. But lo and behold, this little house cat's confidence was through the roof. Nothing in its head told it even for a split second that it couldn't defend itself and its owner's property. The stare-down lasted for over a minute, each stalking the other. Then the cat released a lightning-quick paw strike to the alligator's face, and the gator spun around and ran like hell back into the water.

The point of the story is that confidence comes from practice, determination, and a never-back-down will and persistence to improve.

There's no room for hacks at Confidence Camp. Think of all the mice and birds that cat had probably stalked, and just how much patience that took, or the dozens of dogs it had probably stared down before the alligator turned up. The cat had likely had plenty of practice. That cat kicked the alligator's ass because it was confident. The cat did the work, put in the hours.

Life is a confidence game. How you live it is your choice. And if you hold onto your choices for long enough, they become a state of mind, a way of life. PMA is all about confidence—the confidence to win at any cost because you, like that cat, have put in the work. Confidence is the be-all and end-all. And I'm not referring to the false-ego bolstered confidence here. That's not confidence. I'm talking about the confidence that's based on knowing who you really are, which starts with putting in the work to discover who you are, remaining willing to learn, trying new ways of doing things, and getting better at what you're doing. This is hard work and requires humility. Sounds counterintuitive, but the kind of confidence I'm talking about is based on humility. It takes years' of work and a constant willingness to invest in self-truth. That's the way you get the air of confidence about you, and the catch-22 is you don't go around waving a flag in your own honor. You stay grounded and humble because you *are* grounded and humble.

That's why when kids are having confidence issues and being bullied, I tell parents to take them to the dojo. Have them learn martial arts. They'll develop a skillset that will bring confidence. Martial arts teaches its students to respect themselves and others, to stay humble, to bow out of respect and confidence, not fear.

My nephew and godson Blaise became an amazing young man because he spent his early years in the dojo learning these secrets. Now he walks with his chin up, but he's humble and always ready to help others. Trust me, he's a badass black belt who spars in MMA with dudes twice his age and comes out on top. As a matter of fact, some kids in his high school actually tried to bully him because he was quiet. Blaise warned them he was a black belt and didn't want to hurt them, "but I will if you attack me." Well, those kids looked at some videos on YouTube of Blaise fighting in the cage and that was the end of the bullying.

So my message is this: pay your dues, get better at whatever it is you're doing, and develop your skills. Real confidence is a by-product of hard work, and when you get it, you become like that cat. Then if you ever end up face to face with a situation like that cat and the 'gator, you'll have the same outcome as the cat. Confidence for the win!

When That Cheese Gets Moved

Now, before the vegan social justice warriors with a stick up their ass come hunt me down, let me say that I don't eat cheese. That's not what this is about. What I'm referring to is a great book called *Who Moved My Cheese,* by Spencer Johnson.

The cheese in his book represents what we want in life, our idea of what will make us happy. For some that's career, for others it's spiritual growth, PMA, fitness, family, money, a mansion, a new car—whatever. It's also about what happens when we lose what we have in life. Spencer used the analogy of a mouse in a maze looking for the cheese—not so different from what we humans look for when we spend time in our own maze of groups, organizations, and relationships.

The whole thing boils down to one's ability to be adjust to changing circumstances and loss. As I said earlier, when we're resilient we develop new muscles and new neurons that keep us wired to the moment.

Resilience keeps us flexible, young, on our toes, able to tackle new obstacles with enthusiasm.

When you're able to do that, a whole world of opportunities awaits. We *do* want to leave our bad qualities—negativity, resistance, and self-doubt—on the road behind us, right?

Well, in order to do that we have to remain open to traveling new roads, even ones we're unsure of, that may be intimidating. Change is always uncertain. That's why it's natural to want to resist it. But if we truly want to grow, then we have to break away from our conditioned responses and find new ways. We have to look for new directions, get uncomfortable, embrace the suck, as the Marines say. If you go for it, there will inevitably be some sort of loss along the way.

And so the fear. There's an old expression: "You want to have your cake and eat it too." But we can't. We have to let things go. We have to surrender to triumph. Sometimes the loss will be of friendships. Say you choose to get sober. What would you be afraid of? Perhaps losing your social status? That you'll be alone because all your friends drink? But if those friendships revolve only around getting high or drunk, then they're anchoring you to a life you no longer want. Narcotics Anonymous has it right: people, places, and things—if any of those three revolve around intoxication, you'll have to let it go. Besides, some time alone to face yourself is vital in really comprehending who the hell you are. That's what most people fear—facing that truth.

And, if you make the changes, the people who see you as that new person will find you. There's a whole new group of positive friends out there waiting. I know—I found them. I have made many new friends since I began trying to fix myself.

My circumstances always forced me to live with a constantly changing paradigm. I was never allowed to get comfortable. Whenever I did, bam! Here comes the next curve ball—a whole new set of circumstances. Honestly, those times in my childhood have helped me deal with change as an adult, even change accompanied by great loss. Change has made me more resilient. The fact is, this material world is constantly changing, so we should expect change. Krishna says in the Bhagavad Gita, "Time I am, the great destroyer of the worlds." We can't fight change; we have to embrace it. Learn to see your life philosophically. It will change your perspective. Things I once saw as negative events I now realize had to happen. And I appreciate what I learned from them.

What you should take away from this is the idea that change is going to happen and that new opportunities are found in that change. New cheese, so to speak. So again, go back to that corkboard and map out some things you'd *like* to change and then go for it. Plot your course like a mouse in a maze hell-bent on finding that cheese. Be all in. Engage your mind, senses, intelligence and, most importantly, your spirit, fully in that change. You'll be pleasantly surprised at what you can accomplish. Things will change quickly for you. To the degree we surrender to change, to that degree we'll reap the rewards. It's up to you, though—as long as you stay resilient and open to a changing paradigm, you can and will achieve your goals.

I Order You Fuckers To Laugh

I have to say that people with no sense of humor (along with religious fanatics, political psychopaths, and people who say they don't like music) scare the living shit out of me.

The fact is, laughter breaks up a lot of tense, fucked-up moments and is good for the soul. I credit having a sense of humor to surviving everything I had to go through. Even as kids, while my two brothers and I were getting the shit beat out of us every day, working like slaves, starved, forced to eat dog food and worse by our evil foster family, we always seemed to find ways to joke about most of what was happening to us. Like I said, laughter's a survival skill.

Example: we were only allowed to bathe twice a month because our scumbag foster parents didn't want to run up their water bill. All the foster kids had to use the same bathwater. Think about how nasty that was if you were the sixth one to get into the tub. We also had to maintain *some* level of dignity so that we weren't further picked on at school for being "the dirty orphans." What I did was heist the key to the local gas station bathroom. Then every other morning or so, on the way to school, we'd sneak into that filthy, disgusting bathroom, strip off our clothes, and lather up with the greasy bar of soap on the sink. The three of us would dance around, singing songs. Laughter and humor were how we coped. They served us well for the entire six-plus years we spent in that foster home hell.

You can't even imagine the difficult road my mother traveled in life. Raped and beaten constantly by my scumbag old man, depressed, suicidal, her kids taken away, two major surgeries, one for her heart and the other her spine, homelessness—laughter also helped her tremendously. To this day she continues to be one funny lady. We've been through hell as a family, but we remained resilient because we had the gift of laughter when things got crazy.

I will never forget what one older woman told me when I was a kid: "When you laugh, the whole world laughs with you, and when you cry, you cry alone." I get it. Everyone goes through bad times. The last thing anyone needs is to constantly hear how your life sucks. Blunt, but sorry, it's the truth. Stop bitching, laugh a little, and change your energy. Shit, I did. No one knew what happened to me as a kid because I kept it secret. Then I wrote my first book, *The Evolution of a Cro-Magnon*. It's chock full of crazy stories and no surprise, it's also very funny.

Many people commented after reading it that they couldn't believe I'd gone through what I had because I seemed so happy. But my happiness is a choice. Don't get me wrong—I've had my moments—but laughter always changed my mood overall along with my mental and physical health. There's medical evidence to back up what I'm saying.

Dr. Lee Berk at Loma Linda University School of Medicine, California, did a study that shows that laughter, happiness, and joy "inspire" the immune system to create white "T" cells, commonly called "happy cells," which help prevent infection. He also found that laughter, as a preventive therapy in diabetes care, raises good cholesterol and lowers inflammation.

Laughter also increases blood oxygen levels and gives you more energy. It boosts immunity, lowers stress hormones, decreases pain, helps prevent heart disease, lowers blood pressure, and more. So I guess it's true what they say—laughter really is the best medicine. But it doesn't only work wonders on the body; it helps your mental state, too, because it brings joy, eases anxiety and fear, relieves stress, improves your mood, enhances your ability to be resilient, and, I'll add, helps you develop PMA.

I enjoy spending time with funny people and I love comedies. Not comedy writers, though! Most seem to be depressed as hell. Robert McKee jokingly told us one day in his writing class that some people he knew were having a party. Someone suggested they invite some comedy writers to brighten things up, "Sure . . . till the paramedics arrive!" Funny and so true of most of the comedy writers I've met.

Do yourself a favor: the next time you're having a bad moment or day, try to laugh it off. The sad truth is, things can always be worse. Things can spiral downward quickly if you let them. So laugh at yourself, too. Shit, I do it all the time. I'm still amazed at what a fuck-up I can be. The dumb things I've said and done. The difference is I don't beat myself up over it anymore. Neither should you when you screw up. Don't take things so seriously.

I was at a friend's house and saw a frame hanging on a wall. It had a small stick in it that said, "Life sucked… and then I took the stick out of my ass." He said his brother had given it to him for his birthday and it was spot on. He laughed like hell, too. So forget the Prozac or any of that shit. You don't need it. What you need is the meds of laughter. Try it. You'll live longer and will certainly make more friends.

Keep That Dream Alive

"If one advances confidently in the direction of his dreams, and endeavors to live the life which he has imagined, he will meet with a success unexpected in common hours."

—Henry David Thoreau

Many years ago I was talking to some people about writing movies, books, and touring with my band. Some people said I should look for a *real* job.

Well, two books later (one released by a major publisher), a screenplay, a new band, and an album, I guess I have a real job after all. See, keeping my kidlike attitude worked.

The fact is, I never stop dreaming and I never stop with the follow-through. That's the difference between a child dreamer and an adult dreamer. As adults we have the facility and wherewithal to actually try to attain what we've pinned to our corkboards. We can take constructive action every day and chip away at the goal. The ups and down and the breakthroughs—all part of the process.

Always seek out and make friends with people who also have the ability to dream and who are going for it.

We need to nurture these types of relationships. I was in a relationship once where the girl was so negative that any time I dared to dream, she shot it down. Even when I got the big record deal I'd been working so hard toward, she didn't congratulate me. The news was met instead with negative, toxic words. She'd quit everything she'd ever started. She was living in a mental hell, and I let her drag me into it. Everyone who cared about me commented on how my attitude—and weight—was changing. I was depressed; I ate like a beast to numb the pain. I ate to the point where it hurt to move. I ballooned. I felt like crap. It took me years to climb out of that hole, but the first clawing upward involved dumping her ass.

You have to be committed to moving forward constantly, moving in the direction of your dreams with unrelenting courage. To do this, constantly monitor your association. I like to use the analogy that if you're rowing a boat out to sea, you don't want your anchor stuck in beach sand. Negative people are worse than anchors. They're like cracks in the hull that will eventually fill your boat with water, dash your dreams on the rocks, and drown you.

I hope I'm getting through to you on this point because it's serious business. Always be aware of the destination and goals you've assigned yourself. I mean, keep them always in your mind. Then somehow or other, stay inspired to attain them. Positive relationships are key to maintaining your inspiration and fear is your biggest obstacle. But fear is in the mind. Those who can't quiet the enemy mind and push past it remain paralyzed and in turn may even try to paralyze others. Having dreams energizes your life. It brings a daily sense of PMA. But it has to start somewhere. So get the corkboard, get a journal, and fill the pages with hopes, dreams, and plans.

In his science fiction novel *Dune,* Frank Herbert creates a mantra to conquer fear: "I must not fear. Fear is the mind-killer. Fear is the little-death that brings total obliteration. I will face my fear. I will permit it to pass over me and through me. And when it has gone past I will turn the inner eye to see its path. Where the fear has gone there will be nothing. Only I will remain."

Someone recently asked me if I kept a journal. Shit, yeah, I do! It's on my computer in a file entitled "Shut the fuck up, Enemy Mind... I'm working here." And to all you macho dudes, it's okay, keeping a journal doesn't mean you're weak or a sissy. What it means is you're writing down your emotions as you work hard. What that does is allow you to monitor success and failure and see where your head was at during those times.

Have you ever watched the motivational speaker, the late Dr. Wayne Dyer, give a talk? I have. I loved that guy. He walked around on stage barefoot, dropping science. On more than one occasion I was dealing with something and caught him on PBS talking about that exact thing, including the know-how what to do about it. Life's funny like that. There's always someone, a messenger, if you will, who turns up right when you need him or her. The energy waves are out there in the universe, and if you tune your receiver to the "growth" frequency, you'll find those people.

When I was listening to Dyer I was dealing with some personal issues. I knew I couldn't go back to where I had been—there was no turning back on my journey. I had set a course and had to follow through. It's like I've embarked on a five-mile ocean swim and it was now longer to swim back to shore than to go on, past the point of no return. The last thing I needed in the deep ocean of life was for fear to paralyze me. I know fear's in the mind, but I'm human, and I feel it. When it comes, it's nice to hear the words of a brilliant teacher. That day, Dyer spoke about dreaming: "One of the huge imbalances in life is the disparity between your daily existence, with its routines and habits, and the dream you have within yourself of some extraordinarily satisfying way of living. Buried within you is an unlimited capacity for creation that's anxious to plant seedlings to fulfill your dreams and your destiny. The absence of balance between dreams and daily routine can reveal itself in symptoms of depression, illness, or anxiety—but it's more often something that feels like an unwelcome companion by your side, which continually whispers to you that you're ignoring something. You sense that there's a higher agenda; your way of life and your reason for life are out of balance. Until you pay attention, this subtle visitor will continue to prod you to regain your equilibrium."

I find this so true.

When I don't go after my dreams, when I ignore them, I'm constantly disturbed. It's me giving into resistance. I can never be happy by doing that.

By continuing to dream and to act on my dreams I've become a much happier and more fulfilled person. I feel great empathy and sadness for those who don't dream a life beyond their current circumstances.

Something Patty Smith recently said between songs at a concert in New York City resonated with me: "We are alive. We have our imagination, our blood, our heart, and our creative impulse." We also have a spirit—a spirit that's calling for us to dream. So have the courage and do it. Go after your dreams with unrelenting determination and joy, as a child does. Never stop believing and pushing forward. Never rest on your past laurels, satisfied with what you've achieved thus far. Satisfaction is the death of desire.

My World... My Rituals

I have them before I hit the stage—I burn incense, listen to Bob Marley, stretch, chant mantras, and focus on what I'm about to do.

Before Ironman races it's no different—I set out all my gear, eat the same thing (oatmeal with almond butter and fruit), then walk and chant on my meditation beads near the water. I need Neptune in my corner to help me get through that 2.4-mile swim.

As a matter of fact, I just finished the hardest Ironman I've ever attempted. It was my second time in Kona Hawaii at the 2017 Ironman World Championship. I had to deal with insane heat, crazy winds, rolling hills and hours of solitude out there on the Queen K Highway. I put in a decent 2.4 mile open water swim and was about to PR on the bike course. Then just shy of the 80 mile marker the stabbing pain in my right side began. It was unbearable. After the 112 miles on the bike I got to T2 (transition area bike to run) and it continued, even getting worse. I put my running shoes, blocked out my Enemy Mind and hobbled onto the run course. As I hit the first aid station three miles in the vomitting started. Projectile vomitting in fact and it didn't stop for the entire 26.2 mile marathon. I threw up over twenty times, couldn't keep fluids down and my hands swelled to three times their size. My feet swelled as well. My head pounded, my body ached and I hurt from head to toe. But I never thought for a single moment about quitting. I walked and ran the marathon and crosssed the finish line with my head up and tears in my eyes.

Truth be told, you would have had to carry my ass off that course before I quit. See, I was also racing for Alexander Owens, a very brave 4 year old boy with a deadly disease called, "NF". I found out later that many athletes got sick because the week of heavy rain prior to race day had washed sewage into the swim course which we had trained in all week. Yep, it was a stomach virus and I attribute finishing that race to the fact I had done my rituals that morning, and so I was prepared mentally to accomplish my goal. They put me in a different mindset and took me to a place where I knew there was no room for complacency.

Many of the world's best athletes have rituals as well. Case in point: the greatest professional basketball player of all time, Michael Jordan—did you know that while leading the Chicago Bulls to six NBA championships, the five-time MVP wore his University of North Carolina shorts under his uniform without fail during every game?

People do rituals with the intention of achieving what they set out to do.

Rituals enhance people's confidence in their abilities, motivate them to greater efforts, and improve performance.

Now, I'm no psychologist, but I can speak to what I know to be true, and that is that my rituals take me off the mundane platform, silence the Enemy Mind, and help me tap into an unlimited power source. From that place I don't doubt the outcome even for a minute.

I suggest you find your rituals and give it a try. Doesn't matter what those rituals are or what other people think of them. They're for you and you alone. Your rituals let you know that shit is about to get real. They put you in a warrior's mindset.

Teamwork Works

There's strength in numbers, so surround yourself with people interested in what you're interested in. Schedule training and other events around a team. Then you're not alone and are therefore less likely to flake.

If I have to cycle on a cold-ass day and there are people waiting for me at the 59th Street bridge, there's no way in hell I'm not showing up. I can't let my friends down. Remember, a single stick can be snapped, so join the bunch.

There's a reason the military pushes teamwork and unit integrity on recruits. It's not just about one soldier making it home from the battlefield; it's about the unit making it home. You fight for the person next to you. I've talked to guys who have years of combat experience. They've each said that when the real shit hit the fan and the bullets were flying, it wasn't their country's flag that motivated them to fight like hell; it was the guys next to them—those with whom they'd trained for years. These men had played with each others' kids, loved one another like brothers. The bonds they'd developed through teamwork made them willing to do whatever it took for all of them to make it home. That type of camaraderie brings out the best in people.

You may not be under attack in Fallujah, but even in your day-to-day life, surrounding yourself with others who have similar interests and are willing to work hard to achieve similar goals has great benefits. There's a special energy to that collective spirit of people uniting to achieve something. Big companies like Google do it. They facilitate teamwork by holding retreats and seminars and group consultations on projects along with meditation workshops or other such group activities because teams produce results.

I come from the New York Punk/Hardcore scene—been in it since 1977, when I was just a kid. I never really had a family in the true sense of the word, so these people became my tribe. I've seen this community of people do many amazing things over the years, including helping people get sober, playing benefit shows to cover medical bills for someone with cancer, replacing stolen gear, and spreading the worldwide movement of PMA, veganism and positive change among the youth.

I owe this music scene a great debt. I survived the downsides of the music scene in general because I always tried to hang around the positive peeps and work as a team. That's helped steer me to what I'm doing today. I look around this worldwide scene and I can tell you one thing for sure: these are the real thinkers in society. They're up on all the knowledge, so they'll be the ones to effect real change on the planet in years to come. I'm very proud to know so many of them and share our collective passion for health, fitness, a compassionate diet, PMA, and philosophy, but the only way any of this has developed is because we've worked together. Teamwork.

> **Don't think you can go it alone in life. You can't. The pressures of the day-to-day bullshit will snap you like a twig. Develop friendships and work in teams.**

Confide in one another. Develop trust and unit integrity. That team helped lift me out of the world of shit I was in.

It doesn't matter what you're dealing with, if you look for a group of individuals who have made it their business to overpower and overcome negative influences, you'll succeed. The worst mistake you can make when times are hard is to isolate yourself. **DON'T DO IT!** I too have been given this powerful instruction over the years, so I'm passing it on. All you have to do is get your ass on that PMA train, work in a team, and you'll slowly come out of whatever it is that's going on.

Reset Your Clock—
Get Regulated

I conducted a one-week experiment a little while back: I got up two hours earlier than I normally do (which is already pretty early), and just started my day.

Of course, getting up that early required me getting to bed earlier so I was well rested, and my eating habits also had to change—no late dinners, earlier breakfasts. The amount of work I got done by noon was incredible. As a matter of fact, I liked the by-products of my experiment so much that I've stayed with it. It's helped me become much more productive in all areas of my life.

Fact: The body is designed to function with the progression of the day from sunrise to high noon to sunset. The fire of digestion even works with the phases of the sun. That is, it's strongest at midday. Therefore that's when you should eat your heaviest meal.

Regulating your eating and sleeping is essential. When you do, your body will work like a well-oiled machine.

When I was a monk, they told us constantly to "stay regulated." That meant waking at the same time each morning, showering, meditating or other spiritual practices, eating (and keeping that simple), exercising, studying, service... Then repeat it the next day, and the next. I'm telling you from my own experience that being with the program for close to three years in the early '80s paid off, and I still carry the benefits of that physical and mental routine to this day.

Give it a try. Get to bed a little earlier and then rise a little earlier. Turn off the TV earlier. Get off the internet. Stop checking your Facebook page at 1:30 in the morning to see who talked shit on your latest upload. Then use the time you reclaim to reset your clock, maybe read a book, exercise a little, be creative, tackle the thing you've been putting off, spend more time with your kids—whatever. You'll see day by day that things will get done. You'll accomplish goals and be in a better mood. Your attitude will change in all areas of life.

So unless you work the night shift, get your ass out of bed early. Enjoy a sunrise. Watch the day evolve as the **three modes of nature** flow through the day—morning, goodness; afternoon, passion; night, ignorance. I monitor the modes every day living in NYC. It's calm before sunrise (the Vedas call those early hours the *brahma-muhurta*). Then the sun rises and all of a sudden, here comes the insanity, with honking traffic, yelling people, and all kinds of chatter and other mindless noise. That ratchets up through the day until at night, the intoxicated step out, make bad choices, fight, vomit, and piss all over my block. That's why they say nothing good ever happens after midnight, the witching hour. You can remove so much unnecessary bullshit, drama, and negativity simply by extricating yourself from that so-called nightlife.

Resetting your clock and staying regulated will reset your mood; it'll give you PMA throughout your day. You'll eventually rise above the three modes of nature to the spiritual realm, but in order to do that you first have to come to the mode of goodness, and the mode of goodness requires getting up early and staying regulated, along with meditating, being mindful, exercising, and eating foods that are in the mode of goodness—not products of violence, for example, exercising—all of these work in tandem to help you evolve.

I mean, that's the goal of this book, right, to evolve? As I said, PMA isn't the be-all and end-all of life, but it's a great place to start—something you need in order to progress.

But there's so much more to becoming your very best self than that. What really counts is personal growth in the truest part of you, the soul. Make no mistake, when you reset your clock and regulate your daily activities, you are fast-tracking toward that bigger goal. It shows your Higher Power that you care, that you're making a serious effort. As it's said, "When you take one step toward Krishna [or your path], Krishna takes a thousand steps toward you."

First move is yours, though. Start by resetting your clock and getting into a mode-of-goodness routine. Don't piss away this human form of life. It's a gift. Be grateful for it. Your human body is the vehicle that will take you, its driver, to some pretty amazing destinations.

On that note I'll leave you with this verse from the timeless *Bhagavad-gita As It Is,* along with the purport written by His Divine Grace A. C. Bhaktivedanta Swami Prabhupada. It's from the second chapter, "Contents of the Gita Summarized," text 69. I've included the Sanskrit transliteration:

ya nisha sarva-bhutanam
tasyam jagarti samyami
yasyam jagrati bhutani
sa nisha pashyato muneh

"What is night for all beings is the time of awakening for the self-controlled; and the time of awakening for all beings is night for the introspective sage."

Purport: There are two classes of intelligent men. The one is intelligent in material activities for sense gratification, and the other is introspective and awake to the cultivation of self-realization. Activities of the introspective sage, or thoughtful man, are night for persons materially absorbed. Materialistic persons remain asleep in such a night due to their ignorance of self-realization. The introspective sage remains alert in the "night" of the materialistic men. The sage feels transcendental pleasure in the gradual advancement of spiritual culture, whereas the man in materialistic activities, being asleep to self-realization, dreams of varieties of sense pleasure, feeling sometimes happy and sometimes distressed in his sleeping condition. The introspective man is always indifferent to materialistic happiness and distress. He goes on with his self-realization activities undisturbed by material reactions.

Hit A Home Run Daily

I just played a concert in San Diego. A friend, who's a Navy SEAL, came out with his son before the show and we talked. Well, mostly he talked and I listened. That's what you do when you're around those types—you pick their brains.

My friend had just come off multiple overseas deployments, where he was a team leader. That means not only was he responsible for himself but he had to keep his entire team of badasses working as a unit, fired up, ready to go at a moment's notice. Trust me, you don't get to be a team leader in the SEALs unless you have certain qualities. They include the ability to work through any situation and not lose your shit. You can't; you have other men counting on you.

Anyway, he was telling me his current life philosophy: hit a home run every day. He broke it down to bases. First base means he gets up and trains with his men. Second base means he takes care of things he needs to do for work. Third base he trains in combat sports (BJJ/Muay Thai), and home plate means he goes home and works on his relationship with his wife and kids.

If you want to be like great men, you do what great men do and you do it daily. You don't make excuses; you get it done.

People who make excuses don't get anywhere in my friend's line of work. So step up to the plate, bat in hand, and take a big swing.

Learn From the Past

We all screw up and make mistakes. That's part of life. To err is human. As long as you learn from your mistakes, you're better because you made them.

If you know something is going to bite you on the ass, you should have better sense, but if you didn't, pay more attention next time. Remember those three classes of intelligence? Most of us have to get burned a few times before we learn not to touch the flame.

No decision should be made recklessly. That's why these days when something comes up that I've seen before, I look at my past in order to choose the correct action in my present. Philosopher George Santayana writes that if you don't remember your past, you're doomed to repeat it. Very true. You should know, though, that when you do things with full knowledge of what went wrong the last time, and yet you consciously make the same mistake again, the lessons you'll be taught on the second round will likely be a bit heavier. That's how karma works, and believe me it's real.

So the best advice on making decisions is to weigh in on your past experiences. If you don't have any in a certain area, talk to someone who does. You can learn from the pasts of others, too. If I know someone who was living large, making cash money dealing drugs, and then was sent to prison for ten years, guess what, I'm not going to be selling drugs any time soon. Don't be that person who, after screwing up, says, "Damn, I wish I could go back and change what I did." Travel back in time *before* you take action. Understand from previous mistakes as well as the correct decisions you've made—those that brought you the desired result in a way that didn't compromise your integrity. Looking to the past is how you shape a positive future.

Stay Bulletproof

In this age of social media smack-talking, people are always going to pop shit, lie, criticize, find fault, and direct it right at you.

Now, instead of getting into a war of words or worse, going old school and throwing them a beating, practice one of the Four Agreements: don't take things personally. Their smack talk is their poison. It can only affect you if you let it. These days I'm like, "Let the bullets fly, fuckers. I can take anything you can fire at me."

Why? Because I work on myself to become a better person every day, trying to learn and improve. My day is consumed by that—literally filled with positive action. I have amazing relationships and interact with amazing people. That's not by accident, either. As I said, years ago I chose to surround myself with those who want to help others instead of putting them down.

No time for crumb-bums or their poison. As don Miguel says, they're simply projecting their own hell onto you. Their words illuminate their own darkness. Insecure people project; that's what they do.

I know many of you reading this, like me, have a tendency to take matters into your own hands. Don't. The universe is keeping score, trust me, so let it.

It's not your job to dish out the karma. Everyone gets exactly what they deserve in this life and the next.

Your job, my job, is to not let what people say ruin our days, weeks, months, years. I've grown exponentially on my path since I've been able to let shit go and not care what the crows have to say. Everyone knows that crows gather where the garbage is, so let them enjoy the stank. You be like Superman: bulletproof.

Invest in Sweat Equity

In the late '80s, when I'd just gotten over my crack-pill-booze addictions, I ended up working construction in New York City. The guy I worked for, Robin, was a 6'6" black belt badass in karate, studying under a guy named Kayo. It was one of Kayo's students who wrote *The Karate Kid*.

Robin got up at the crack of dawn, hit his gong, chanted his Buddhist mantras, took his kids to school, did hard manual labor all day long, then trained for hours at the dojo. I was renting a room in his space on 6th Street in those days, so I saw all this drive firsthand.

One of the things he preached was "sweat equity." You have to invest in what you want and be willing to bust your ass to get it. His hustle was insane. Even on job sites, katas were taught on breaks. There was no slacking, not ever. He said you had to produce, because if you didn't you were off his crew. It was that simple. He played no favorites. It wasn't a popularity contest, and he didn't give a shit who you were. Produce or go home.

See, Robin knew one very important factor in business as well as and in life: there are people out there going after the same things we want. The competition was hustling, training, bidding on the same jobs, willing to work hard. So he knew the only way to get a leg up was to outwork them, to invest more sweat, to be relentless in his drive and ambition. If he knew his competition was going to get up at 6 a.m., he was up at 5:30. They worked ten-hour days? He's putting in twelve. They played ball after work? He'd play three full-court games, then go chant and do two hours of martial arts. He was one of the most tenacious, driven people I knew back then, and I respected the hell out of him for that. I learned so much being around him right at a time when I was coming out of some really bad shit.

The point I'm making here is that when your Higher Power sees you're willing to invest sweat equity, things manifest.

They did for Robin and for me as well. When I opened a yoga center on St. Marks some years back that fed people and gave free classes and books, all Robin's lessons paid off. I had a construction business of my own at the time, and I went to work every day. Then I went to build the yoga center after work and ran a crew. I'd sweat my ass off, sleep three or four hours a night, even work out, but I was never tired. My spiritual battery was charged. I knew what had to be done and I did it. I also did it with PMA—never complaining.

I had a few slackers volunteering, but I made them work their asses off too. And why did they do it? Because I was right there sweating next to them, working harder than they were. I was driven—invested 1,000 percent—for the entire six months it took us to build the center. A surfer friend commented, "It was the worst and the best time of my life." Yeah, I made him give up those big-swell days when he wanted to drive out to Rockaway Beach with his surfboard. But in the end, when the center was finished and filled with the people we were helping, he knew every drop of sweat he'd invested had been worth it.

I live by the code to not half-ass my life. I mean, think about it: who are you really getting it over on anyway? You'll be weeded out by someone or by circumstances. The man or woman next to you will outwork you, outsweat you, and you'll be gone. Don't let that happen. Go after what you want with relentless drive, *dridha-vrata,* and do it with a clear head. Remember the mantra, "Intoxication destroys determination." God is omnipotent. He knows the exact number of drops of sweat you've invested in what you're doing. Don't slack. Work hard every damn day. Be all in and sweat, my friends.

See Adversity as a Blessing

"Every adversity has the seed of an equivalent or greater benefit."
—Napoleon Hill

When I was a kid in that foster home, then alone on the streets, then locked up, I couldn't figure out why all that was happening to me. What the hell had I done to deserve it?

I don't ask those questions anymore. I know those experiences were part of my journey. Adversity builds character, and true character is only revealed under pressure. The choices I made when times were tough defined who I am today, mistakes and all. My realizations on that are twofold. First, I now know that I was working out some past-life karma. I was not a victim. I owed myself that suffering and the healing that followed it. Second, in the process I gained so much firsthand knowledge of suffering and climbing out of it that I'm now able to pass it on to others who are going through their own karma. You too pay it forward.

So if you're dealing with adversity, welcome the ride and do what it takes to work through it.

Recognize the test, that it's your moment to shape both your character and your future. Don't look for sympathy like a victim. To be brutally honest, no one really cares. They have their own set of adverse circumstances going on. We all do. Take my advice and see the blessing that is your life. It's all a matter of perspective. Use what you have to advance on your journey.

Out of everything I've told you in this book, this is it: if you can develop this type of perspective in your day-to-day dealings, you're going to achieve amazing things. You'll get your shit done under any and all circumstances. And that wonderful childhood baggage (yes, we all have it) will be left curbside for the trash man. Once I flipped the script on my baggage—when I saw things for what they were and stopped playing the blame game—good things began to manifest. Was it easy? Hell, no. But I wanted more out of life and needed to change in order to get there. My change was dependent, actually, on developing this perspective.

So the next time you're dealing with adversity, when you're down in the muck, think about that Napoleon Hill statement I quoted up top. Meditate on it. Remember it. You'll be served very well by doing so.

Your Mind Is Faster Than You Are

Back when I first started my awakening in the early '80s, I bounced all over the place—from this ashram to that one, from New York to Puerto Rico, Puerto Rico to Hawaii, Hawaii to New York again. Things would come up and off I'd go. That's when one of the older devotees in the ashram told me that no matter where I went on this planet, I would be taking my mind with me. Man, was he right.

I just met up with a friend in L.A. who's dealing with this exact same point. In the last seven years he's moved to and from NYC twice, to Florida, back out west to L.A., and now, he says, he's moving back to NYC. He's always agitated, has no peace of mind, and can't focus. He's a great musician, but he can't even get his act together to write an album. He's even changed his profession several times. It's always the same story—something went down and he had to move on to the next thing.

> **No matter how fast you move, your mind will move faster. You can't leave it behind. It will haunt you.**

Whatever issues you have going on in one place will be there to greet you when you arrive in a new place. It's a pretty safe bet that those issues originated on the mental platform. That's why you have to stay put, stand your ground, and deal with things head-on. The Gita says an uncontrolled mind can be your worst enemy. The only way to conquer the mind is to bring it under the control of the higher self by constant mindfulness, meditation, and tons of practice.

One of the practices I do is to be conscious that I'm not the mind but separate from it. The mind is a subtle energy, like the intelligence and ego. We say "My mind," right? In 1981, when I started my yoga practice, I attended the Integral Yoga Institute. Before each class the teachers instructed us to do this chant: "Not the body, not the mind, eternal self I am." Actually, this has to be drilled into our heads. We've been conditioned since birth to identify with the mind and body. And so we suffer. Mental suffering is the worst. It can be paralyzing. That's why that older devotee kept telling me, "Hey, John, you need to get off the mental platform!"

Only when I began to practice seeing myself as above the mind did I begin to find peace. You can too. Just take time during your day to do an internal inventory. Stay centered. Monitor the desires the mind is feeding you. Will they serve the higher self or drag you down to the depths of some mental hell or other? And remember that no matter where you run, the Enemy Mind will be waiting for you. If there's conflict between higher and lower selves, stand your ground as the higher self and fight.

Prioritize Your Goals

This is where you go back to your corkboard and make adjustments. Prioritize your goals according to long- and short-term by rating them on a scale of 1 to 10. Which are most the most urgent to achieve right now?

An example, in my opinion, of an immediate one: sobriety. I'd make that number 1. Changing your diet would be number 2. That means that the book idea you've had in your head for a few years or the race you've been itching to run may have to settle a little farther down the page. It's up to you, of course—where you're at in your life. If you're already a clean and sober plant-based athlete, obviously your goal list will have a different set of priorities than the list of someone who's struggling with sobriety and a toxic diet.

Also, ask yourself which goals you think about constantly. Putting things off and giving into resistance is a sure-fire way to give you a run of shitty days. I'm speaking from experience here. It could be something as mundane as not accomplishing a goal I set to organize my papers. The Enemy Mind looks for the slightest crack in our armor to burrow through.

Setting goals and prioritizing them comes down to time and circumstance. Which ones do I need in the moment?

How important are each of them? Do they fall in line with the core values I've established for my life these days? Which can I commit the most energy to right now? Which goals can I achieve without others' help? Relying on others to get things done can let you down sometimes, so I make sure that many of both my short- and long-term goals don't depend on needing someone to help me. I try to have as much control as I can over my goals' execution and outcome.

Another important thing to ask yourself: why did you choose a particular goal? Are you motivated by ego—so you can somehow prove yourself better than someone else? Or is it related to a burning, heartfelt desire for self-improvement. If you choose goals with a "lower" motivation, your commitment to them will fade down the road. Staying committed through the ups and downs will be checked if your reason isn't true and filled with integrity. Most of the people who choose egocentric goals give up, and giving up on goals is one way to crush your self-esteem. So always ask yourself, "Why do I want to do this?"

We never know what the outcome will be once we've achieved a goal, but I can tell you one thing for sure, seeing things through to the end and completing goals will open new doors for you. You'll learn a lot about yourself. That's why I always have new goals. I finish a race—I sign up for the next one. A book—what's the next one about, John? Setting goals and prioritizing them will keep you moving forward in a positive direction, and that, my friends, is the essence of a positive, fulfilling life.

Change your World

Every day you're lucky enough to open your eyes is a chance for you to make a statement about the direction of your life thought by thought, word by word, action by action. If you want to make changes in your world, start on the subtle level and work out from there.

I mean, the entire change process starts with a desire in the mind. You have to meditate on how you want things to be and then take the appropriate actions. That's why *The PMA Effect* is so vital to your process. The attitude with which you think, speak, and act is crucial.

The circles in which I've run over the past forty years have exposed me to a lot of people who are trying to overcome some pretty bad things, including addiction, childhood trauma, depression, even suicidal thoughts. Unfortunately, there are those who weren't able to overcome their circumstances. That's just real life—real talk. I will say this, though: the ones who pushed through all shared a similar mindset, had a particular quality about them. That is, they desired to heal so bad it hurt. They wanted to change their lives so badly that they never let anything or anyone get in their way.

That's what it takes. You have to want it, and you must constantly remember and learn from your past mistakes. When tests come, you have to stop, reflect on what the correct decision or path would look like, then (and only then) act. Changing your situation is a daily effort, and it requires proper decision-making every step of the way. Don't act impulsively; think things through all the way to their end as far as you are able to.

I just saw an episode of "Locked up Abroad," and this guy got over twenty years in one of the worst prisons in Thailand for smuggling ten kilos of heroin. The prison was full of psychopaths, who tried daily to kill him. He slipped into a depression, then madness. Finally, he broke and decided to kill himself the slow way by going on a hunger strike.

He didn't eat anything for over a month. He was fading. Then a Muslim inmate sat outside his cell every day and told him he had no right to do what he was doing. A week later, other Muslim inmates began to pray outside his cell. Forty days into the fast, the prisoner couldn't see—his eyes stopped working. He could only see with his mind, and so he began to meditate. It was then that he decided he wanted to live and needed to change his world. He became a Muslim and meditated and prayed every day. Two decades later, he was pardoned by the Thai government and extradited to the U.S. to serve another prison sentence. Still, he stayed on the path.

At the end of the show we see him sitting on a cliff overlooking the ocean in his home country, Australia. He spoke of his realizations about the hell he'd gone through. Reflecting brought all the pain back, and we can see the tears welling up in his eyes and hear his voice choking up. It was a real moment. He said everything he'd been through, everything that had brought him to those hellish places, was his own doing. It was his fault. The bad choices he'd made day after day, the seemingly insignificant things that had led him to such major changes. That's how the Enemy Mind cons us—little by little, piece by piece, until we're in a world of shit.

When he was on the brink of death in Thailand, starving himself to death, he realized, through his mindfulness practice, that he was responsible for his suffering, and he decided to change his world. Despite his awareness of that, he remained in prison for most of his life. Still, he changed his perspective and found meaning. Hopefully we can learn something from his story. I know I did, not the least of which is that I never want to end up in that world. Like him I have to make the proper choices every day. If I want to change my world for the better, I'll have to start that change during those subtle moments when I'm training my mind.

The medieval bhakti text *Sri Upadeshamrita*, translated as *The Nectar of Instruction,* notes that one of the qualities of spiritual practitioners is that they're willing to reveal their minds in confidence—they accept help. Never try to go it alone, because you'll lose that fight. If you are having bad thoughts and desires, stay around people who are positive and can help you, those who have already changed their world or at least are in the midst of doing it. Those people know the tricks the mind will use. Tell them what's going on. Don't isolate yourself. That's how we stay strong. Like the men who gathered around the hunger-striking prisoner and became his team, we too need a team.

Take that Shot

"We miss 100 percent of the shots we never take."

—*Wayne Gretzky*

We've talked about prioritizing goals. Even more important, though, is taking action, because if you don't take the shot, you can't catalyze change. I know quite a few people who got so caught up in the mental game, trying to figure out all the variables, that they never took the first step, so opportunity passed them by.

Others just go for it. No fear of failure. They understand that any opportunity not taken is an opportunity lost. So true.

I will go one step further and say that success favors the brave.

Now, that's not to say we should act all willy-nilly and go at things unprepared. No, we have to position ourselves in order to take that shot for success, and positioning means preparation. Your preparation will determine how well you'll be able to take your *best* shot. Being prepared also reduces the fear factor. When I show up prepared at an Ironman starting line for the 2.4-mile swim, I'm better able to stay calm and to visualize that finish line.

It definitely takes courage to take a shot at a goal. You expose yourself to ridicule. You have to get past that. *You're* the warrior stepping into the arena willing to shed blood, sweat, and tears. It's not the critics doing that. Critics don't do jack shit. Most critics are failures. Failures are often envious. You just can't worry about what others think. Just always do your best. Prepare yourself as best you can and go for it.

Remember to stay consistent. To improve your ability when you're taking the shot means constantly *working* to improve, and that comes from discipline and determination. Staying open to new ways and always learning is also vital, as we've discussed. That's how you create opportunities. Not many succeed in just one shot. It's consistency and a willingness to be unafraid of failure that yields the best harvest.

Have a Beautiful Obsession

Obsession by definition means "An idea or thought that continually preoccupies or intrudes on a person's mind."

Unfortunately, most people attach a negative connotation to the word. However, the reality is that being obsessed with one's endeavors, if those endeavors have value, is imperative to achieving your goals.

For example, take the writing of this book. I've been at it for over two years. I'm consumed by it. I wake up and write. I have an experience during the day and jot down a note about it so I remember to use it in the book. Every bit of spare time I have I'm at the computer. I think about it all through dinner, when I'm watching a movie, and right before my eyes close at night. It's "What will I write tomorrow? How can I improve what I've already written? Did I give it my best effort today? If not, I'll do better tomorrow."

If that's not obsession I don't know what is. But it's a healthy obsession. What makes it healthy is my hope and my intent that this book will meet the goal I set for it: it will help someone. I mean, the writing process has helped me tremendously in my day-to-day living. All the positive feelings that came as a result of doing the work, and all the digging deep and reflecting on some really bad stuff and how it made me feel—it was an austerity. If you remember, we defined *austerity* earlier as doing something hard in order to achieve a desired outcome.

So what will your healthy obsession be? How will it drive you?

Maybe it's to eat better, lose that extra twenty pounds, write *your* book, finish a marathon, start that philanthropic endeavor. Whatever it is, fall in love with the process of achieving it. No one has ever achieved anything great without some level of obsession. Actually, positive obsession fuels the creative process. Creativity coach Eric Maisel, PhD, states, "Negative obsessions are a true negative for everyone, but most creators—and all would-be creators—simply aren't obsessed enough. For an artist, the absence of positive obsessions leads to long periods of blockage, repetitive work that bores the artist himself, and existential ailments of all sorts."

Next question: how do we keep healthy obsessions burning? Here are a few suggestions that work for me:

1. **Write your obsession on index cards so it's visible.** Then pin it to your corkboard so it's in your face, a constant reminder of what you need to do. I can visualize mine because I've written it down. My writing teacher says if it's not written down, it doesn't exist. So make it happen, captain, and write it down!

2. **Dramatically cut down the time you spend watching TV and on social media sites.** Trust me, you're not missing anything. I was just in L.A. for a week doing a reading/book signing, and I stayed at a place with no TV. That means there were no news programs pumping negative stories into my brain cells. No constant Big Pharma and poison food ads. Nothing. I even stayed off social media except to post about the events I was doing. I had no time for people's bullshit drama. Let me tell you, that was one of the most productive weeks I've had in months. So give it a try. Become a recluse, in a sense, by creating some silent space around yourself. Live with your obsession undiluted.

3. **Become selective about who's in your social circle.** Time is your most valuable commodity. Don't waste it on bullshit hangouts that won't take you closer to your goal. You also have to "weed out the bugs," as they say in the military. Cut out the negative people completely. Most will try to plant demons of doubt in your Enemy Mind. Only chill with the go-getters, the A-type personalities who'll

instill confidence in you. They know anything's possible if you're willing to apply yourself.

4. **Plan out your days down to the hour. Get a calendar.** I have one. On it I list everything I'll be doing the next day. I plan my days from the moment I wake up until bedtime. There are no days off. When I'm not working my j-o-b, I'm working my obsession—my career. Also, you have to leave room, obviously, for contingencies, because things don't always go as planned. But know what's got to get done. Create a roadmap to success.

5. **Finally, never worry about what others might think or say.** You're weird, you're crazy, you're obsessed—of *course* you're obsessed, but it's a good obsession. Do you know why most people use that word with its negative connotation or find it weird that you're focused, driven, and determined? Because most people are satisfied being mediocre. They fear breaking away from the herd. Taking risks is not who they are. But you—you can be different. You have dreams, yes, obsessions, a desire to achieve something great. So don't be afraid of a little alone time. It has worked for me. Always remember to be yourself. Stay true to the path you've chosen under any and all circumstances. As the great writer Oscar Wilde put it, "Be yourself—everybody else is already taken."

Wake Your Best Wolf

Wolves are fascinating, highly social animals. Their famous howl is actually how they communicate with their packmates and other wolves. They use that howl to gather the pack, defend their territory, maintain social bonds within the pack, and attract mates.

Wolves are extremely motivated by hunger. They wake hungry and can eat anywhere from five to fourteen pounds of meat a day. Nature has designed them to be carnivores. But hunts are only successful 3–14 percent of the time, so they survive on a feast-or-famine diet. They spend 35 percent of their time roaming, traveling twenty to thirty miles a day, but they may cover upwards of a hundred miles in search of prey. And when that prey is in sight, they can run at a speed of almost forty miles per hour in order to pull it down.

I think there's a lot to be learned from a wolf's attitude. Their burning hunger—your goal. Do you wake hungry? Are you willing to endure adversity and stay resilient day after day, even if the object of your desire doesn't manifest immediately? Are you, too, prepared for a feast-or-famine diet? And when the goal is in sight, do you run at top speed, 100 percent focused on your "kill"?

Wolves are also fearless. They'll attack animals much larger than themselves, although of course they hunt in packs. But trust me, wolves carry no dead weight in the pack. You either produce or you hit the bricks. I'd compare that to those we choose for our own pack, our social circle. We've already discussed that association is key. Do you run with the hungry, top-tier, highly motivated "wolves" in your human pack?

If you feel life is passing you by while others are succeeding, time to wake your inner wolf.

Figure out what you want and go after it with relentless determination. You're capable of living the life you want. It only requires a change in attitude. Face what you fear; don't run from it. I do one thing I fear every day. I tackle something that makes me uncomfortable. It's imperative that you're not afraid to face fear. There are no free rides. No one is going to carry you; no one owes you anything. If you want it, you'll have to be fearless and go after it.

You also have to remain flexible because, like wolves, your hunt may only be successful 3–14 percent of the time. Do the wolves quit?

Hell, no—they're top-of-the-food-chain badasses. Many highly successful people will tell you that like in storytelling, there's a gap between expectation and result. They tried something but didn't arrive where they intended. Because they remained flexible and open to change, however, they found another way, and in the end they succeeded.

Rigid humans who go by the book in every aspect of their lives—who need a schematic just to wipe their asses—will quit before the finish line. Flexible people, life's human wolves, will roll with life's punches and drive on to success. They know if they didn't make a kill today, there's always tomorrow. They'll show up day after day and put the work in. It's that relentless forward motion we've been talking about. PMA is not achieved by lazy people with full bellies. Stay hungry!

Get PMA Fit

In bootcamp the military uses three measurements to define a recruit's level of fitness: strength, flexibility, and endurance. So what do you say we run with their model here?

Strength: PMA gives you the strength you need to weather life's storms. You'll develop muscles you never knew you had—muscles that will get you through ups and downs, highs and lows, and allow you to carry loads and finish tasks, never satisfied with mediocrity. You'll always go above and beyond to achieve what you want because you'll have built character, an internal bicep that's done thousands of curls and pull-ups.

Felixibility: Do you know what happens when you keep tightening a muscle, overworking it with heavy loads to the point of fatigue without taking the time to stretch it out? That muscle may be pulled or torn. That's why flexibilty is important. I've learned this the hard way in my training by suffering numerous injuries. Now I stretch all the time. The fact is that PMA will teach you to become flexible in your decision-making, to look at all sides of any equation, to realize that you're not going to be right all of the time. You'll learn to find other ways to do things. Flexibilty will help you with resilience, too. Muscles become resilient and recover quickly when you stretch them before and after you work them. Same deal with the rest of your life.

Endurance: Much like a long-distance runner or an Ironman, endurance is achieved by countless hours of training, pushing through lactic threshholds. Without endurance you can have all the strength and flexibilty you want, but if you're only good for short bursts, you won't get far. That's why developing a positive minsdet is vital. Much like that story of Mark Allen, who kept missing his chance to win the Kona World championship. As soon as he changed his thought process through meditation, he won year after year. Six times, in fact! The military also pushes recruits hard so that they have the endurance to stay in the fight physically as well as mentally. They actually put challenges in Special Ops training in order to teach this principle. Those who can't push through are dropped. As they say, "Most plans never survive the first contact with the enemy." In our case, the enemy is the mind. The mind will attack you relentlessly unless you are strong, flexible enough to change battle tactics when necessary, and are in it for the duration. Life is not a sprint. So work on endurance through PMA and you'll be in it for the long haul. Those who have this attitude simply don't quit. That alone makes them winners.

Make Others Happy

There are so many books being written on how to be happy. Most people find happiness elusive, and those who try to achieve it by conventional means tend to fail miserably.

The reason for this is that their quests are usually self-centered. Sorry, Charlie, but life doesn't work like that. We're both interconnected and interdependent. The "I, me, mine" generation is finding this out the hard way, and trust me, the guys selling the prescription antidepressants are loving what's going on.

I was walking through New York's streets the other day, watching everyone face-down in their cell phones, letting life pass them by completely. We have so much comfort, so many gadgets meant to make life easier in this country, but we're also the most depressed, overmedicated group to ever walk the face of the earth. The esoteric teachings of yoga say the face is the index of the mind. So check out people's faces. Who seems happy? By my own stats, 99 percent of the people out there aren't happy. Sure, they have fleeting moments of happiness, but most of the time they're disappointed. There are many reasons for this, and I believe I've addressed a number of them in this book, but probably the biggest reason is cutting yourself off from others the way our cell-phone society has done to us.

I did a radio show recently. The woman who was hosting asked how I'd ended up with such a kind heart after all I'd been through. I answered in two parts. First, I told her I hadn't always been this way—in fact, I had spent decades angry. But developing and, more importantly, maintaining, PMA got me to where I am presently. Secondly, I became happy by serving others, devoting my energy to trying to make others happy. That has in turn made me a much more happy person.

But that's how the world works.

The more we give, the more we get.

So the answer to modern man's quest for happiness is *not* going to be found in a prescription pill bottle, blunt, beer, hallucinogenic, video game, iPhone, house, car, clothes, or any other temporary bullshit. Real, lasting happiness is found on the path of PMA, and it can be traversed quickly if you use the practice to serve others every day. Give it a shot. Just make sure you do it without expecting anything in return. That will make your kindness selfless. Remember the quote from *Bhagavad-gita As It Is*? We have a right to the work, but we are not entitled to the results.

A Cause Bigger than Yourself

This also comes down to serving others, but on a much larger scale. The higher the level of service, the greater your resilience, because you understand completely that what you're doing isn't just about you.

Not that you develop a Jesus complex or some nonsense like that, but you understand completely what has to be done because you're driven by a higher calling. That gives you passion and purpose.

Holocaust survivor Dr. Viktor Frankl writes, "He who has a *why* can bear any *how*." Did you see the movie *Schindler's List*? It tells the true story of Oskar Schindler, the German industrialist who saved the lives of over twelve hundred Jews from the Nazi death camps by employing them in his factories. Talk about a higher calling. I don't know about you, but I cried like a baby during that film.

Schindler's resolve to save those souls was incredible. He risked his life because had the scumbag Nazis caught him, he would have been executed as a traitor.

When we're connected to something larger than ourselves, it gives us a sense of immortality.

We know that those who are born are sure to die, but the deal is, when we work for a positive cause that will help people into future generations, our acts outlive us. Take, for example, what I and so many others are doing to stop the animal industrialists. That's about saving lives, isn't it? Damn straight. We're working to save the lives of billions of animals and millions of people—not to mention the planet itself. We're working like hell to turn the tide on this bullshit because if we don't, there will be nothing left for our kids or their kids or their kids after them. Not only that, but the vicious cycle of disease in which we currently find ourselves will just continue. Then there's also the by-product of abstaining from flesh-eating to create an evolution in consciousness for our species. That's the cause I've chosen, and it will no doubt outlive me.

Educating people on health, spirituality, and things like beating addiction is what I do. I'm paying it forward because I have a karmic debt. In these causes I've found my higher calling. Having a purpose bigger than myself is so vital to my PMA. Without it I'm lost. We wander through life so unsure of things. The greatest thing we can do is to help others. Nothing else matters. Really. No bullshit. I'm not after fame, money, or adoration in what I do. All those will be useless at the time of death. What natters most to me is reaching out to others.

This book is also an effort to do that. Even if only one person turns his or her life around because of what I've written here, my book will be a success. I'm willing to bet it will help more than one, though—not because I'm so smart, but because the information contained here, information I've gathered over almost four decades, saved my own life.

The upside of serving a cause greater than yourself is that you're never on the losing end of the equation. You develop a sense of community when you take up a cause. You meet new friends, make new acquaintances, most of them positive people with goals similar to yours. Some people have even found spouses among cause participants—people with similar interests and who, like them, are reaching for the mode of goodness.

An example: raising over 97k for my NF Hero, Alexander Owens, through the Children's Tumor Foundation. We did all kinds of fundraisers—10k runs, Brazilian jiu-jitsu events, benefit concerts, online auctions, fitness challenges… I have met so many amazing people through this cause, people with whom I'm still great friends to this day and am lucky as hell to have in my life.

It's also brought me unconditional love for the entire Owens family. I knew going into this cause that that would happen. That's why I did it. As I said earlier, it's okay to be selfish as long as what you're doing will make you a better person. Racing Kona Ironman twice for Alexander, meeting amazing people, and raising both money for and awareness of the disease has definitely done that for me.

So find your calling, your higher cause, and stick with it. Keep it in the center of your day. Be all about it. Be all in.

There is no loss or diminution on the path—there's only unlimited, ever expanding happiness and PMA!

Stay High Forever

I get high. I do it every day. Matter of fact, I get wasted! Oh, and I'm 100 percent clean and sober.

My high doesn't come from poisoning myself with artificial stimulants through in-**toxic**-ation. It comes from things like meditation, chanting mantras, playing music, writing, exercise, yoga, talking philosophy, organic, plant-based meals cooked and eaten with friends, and all the other positive things I do daily.

As Isaac Newton proved, what goes up must come down. That's also true with drugs and alcohol. The crash is hard, and you're always in a worse place afterward.

If you really want to get high—and stay high—work on yourself. PMA will get you there. Expect to sacrifice. The work is, as it says in bhakti philosophy, about removing *anarthas,* unwanted things, or, literally, things that work against your self-interest.

Good things just don't come cheaply. Remember, no *sahajiyas* allowed. *Sahajiyas* take things cheaply.

So if you want *real* enlightenment, which we all do, although only some know it, it'll require sobriety.

No amount of material sense gratification can make you happy. Only the growth of your internal, spiritual dimension can do that. So, yeah, sure, acid or other hallucinogenics might give you a tiny glimpse into another dimension or realm of consciousness, but because it's artificial, you'll end up in a world of shit. You can't touch spirit by standing on matter.

Instead, do the work to find your spiritual self and get high on that enlightenment. Then you'll stay high forever.

Fall in Love with Life

Please, please, please, don't take your life for granted. Life is such a fragile thing. We're here for but a short time, so let's vow to live life to the fullest and go after what we want. If things aren't going according to plan, fix them. Don't complain. Make changes. Look forward to every new day. That's how I roll. I hope you will too.

As I get older, more and more of the people I know are getting sick and passing away. It really sucks. But if I'm to take anything positive away from that loss it's resolve. Some have told me from their deathbeds, "John, go after shit, man. Get everything you want in life. Do it for me, because I can't do it now."

I get choked up even thinking about my friends' final moments. And I will not turn a deaf ear to their words. They implored me to spread whatever knowledge I have, so in my own limited way I'm trying.

I've actually seen a lot of death, but I've also witnessed firsthand all the amazing transformations that so many people have undergone. Many of them even cheated death for the moment by changing their paths. I did that too. But it's why I do what I do. I go to prisons, I mentor kids and adults, and I'll go the extra mile to try to help someone. It's my service in this lifetime. My higher cause. I take NO credit for it. I owe everything to those who have educated me, especially my guru, A.C. Bhaktivedanta Swami Prabhupada, who instructed me in *atma-tattva*—the science of the self. He also told me that Vedic knowledge is meant to deliver us from the suffering and contamination of our connection to matter. If you want to have your mind completely blown, do yourself a favor and read the first ten verses of the Second Canto of *Srimad-Bhagavatam*. When you do, you'll understand why I act with such urgency to help others.

Just today someone thanked me for writing my books because they've changed his life. I told him I am fool #1 and that he should look to the source of any knowledge I've gathered. I also told him he could do that by getting Srila Prabhupada's books. I added, and here are my exact words, "Thank yourself. Yes, I may have written the books, but you, sir, are the one who had the good sense to apply the knowledge contained in them. You did the work, and for that congratulations are in order."

***The PMA Effect* contains decades of lessons from classes down at the University of the Streets.**

I have nothing special that any of you don't have. I just wanted to change my life so badly that I went after it. Please do it too. Walk away from these pages with the determination to get more out of life, to improve yourself, and to pay it forward. Fall in love with your life and live it to the fullest. Face your fears. Stop being afraid of change. Don't stay stuck, paralyzed by a fear of the unknown, of what's waiting around the next turn. Uncertainty is part of life. I was always pushed down uncertain roads. Pushed? Hell, shoved! So here's your nudge.

And stop blaming yourself for past mistakes. Learn from them, yes, but forgive yourself. Be kind to YOU. To quote author Shannon L. Alder, "Accomplishments don't erase shame, hatred, cruelty, silence, ignorance, discrimination, low self-esteem, or immorality. It covers it up, with a creative version of pride and ego. Only restitution, forgiving yourself and others, compassion, repentance, and living with dignity will ever erase the past."

I love that statement because it's so damn true. If you wake up today, let yesterday's faults stay in the past. Don't be haunted by the demons of the past. The Four Agreements, which tell us not to take things personally, applies to all of us. You'll always make mistakes even when you're high on PMA. But you'll get past them as you go around the many learning curves and turn the corner toward uncertainty.

But love your life. That's why PMA is so important—your negative mindset will tell you you're a fuck-up, but the PMA effect tells you to let it go and here's another day to do the right thing.

So push past your doubts and fears. Achieve greatness. Kick your Enemy Mind in the ass. Come on my brothers and sisters, be all in. Turn pro today!

Never Give Up

If you read my first book, *The Evolution of a Cro-Magnon,* you know that in the final words I encourage people to live by the code of the true warrior—meaning, never give up. Me, I never want to be that dude who laments over what could have been had I finished or even just started. Just do your best, be determined, and never quit.

I'm not a great Ironman, but do you know why I took up the sport? Because it teaches me focus, discipline, and most of all, determination. Ironmen don't quit. I quit in Florida because I was unprepared. I became hypothermic and paid the price for it. But I knew right away I had to get back on that horse and I did. Ironman has helped me in so many areas of my life because of what it's taught me: *dridha-vrata,* single-minded determination.

Help yourself. Build good friendships with those who get their shit done and make no excuses.

Do you know the story of Liz Murray? She went from being homeless to graduating from Harvard. Her book, *Breaking Night*, is an amazing read. Both her parents were drug addicts. She talked about eating ice cubes and toothpaste with her sister when they were hungry, because her parents had spent their welfare check on mainlining coke. Her mom died of AIDS when Liz was 15. Her father, who also had AIDS, spent the rent money on drugs until they lost their apartment.

Her sister crashed on a friend's sofa, but Liz was homeless, sleeping on trains and in the streets. She went to school dirty, with lice in her hair, and was bullied. She pushed herself to graduate high school. Then she won a scholarship to Harvard. She was determination personified. She made something out of her life. Liz now works as an inspirational speaker, talking to teenagers about staying away from drugs and not letting hardship hold you back. She's given speeches alongside Tony Blair, Mikhail Gorbachev, and the Dalai Lama. Oprah Winfrey even gave her an award. Just stop and consider how deep she had to reach to do what she did. Talk about the warrior code and PMA.

So whatever you're going through, be patient. It will pass. Under no circumstances should you ever let it stop your relentless forward motion. Everything we've talked about has taught you to see hardships as tests. Being tested at all means the finish line is in sight. Relish your victory when you get there because the struggle made it so much more. That's why many rich kids end up being fuck-ups—they never have to work for anything.

Most of us are different. We had no silver spoons. We've had to shed blood, sweat, and tears to get anything. So feel gratitude and appreciation. Hone your desires and stay hungry. You now have the tools to feed yourself. So thrive on, my friends!

Afterthoughts

What's bugged out is I never intended to write this book. I mean sure, I've always talked about the importance of PMA since I first heard about it from the Bad Brains way back in 1980. But a book? Nah. I'm not one of them self-help, new-age nutjobs telling people how to micromanage their lives right down to the way they wipe their asses in the morning (although I am a left hand front-to-back guy. I'm just saying).

Then came my "gap between expectation and result." As I was going through stuff in my own life that wasn't working out the way I'd anticipated, I began to take shelter of the methods I had learned over the years. I wrote down what I was doing, put it all on my corkboard, and voilà! Two and a half years later, here it is.

Over the past three plus decades, I've given advice to those who sought it from a streetwise New Yorker. I've written songs, books, magazine articles, newspapers, blogs, and spoken for podcasts, radio, and TV shows about my experiences. Shit, I've even been on the spoken word circuit across the globe with people looking to hear about my journey and what it took for me to change.

Everyone loves a great underdog story, and boy did I have one. So as I began patting myself on the back a few too many times, falsely thinking I had it all figured out, the universe, with its impeccable timing, was preparing to throw me a ninety-mile-an-hour curveball exactly when I needed it.

I believe there is a high level of education to be had through hardship, but only if you endure it and look past the false ego.

Only then can we map out a path to happiness, actually become happy, and then stay that way. Unlike these fuckers who've written their countless books on the subject of happiness, are assholes to everyone, and who down three types of antidepressants before breakfast, I have actually achieved some happiness.

I also believe that one of the main factors that contribute to a person living a happy and fulfilled life is setting goals that challenge the depths of his or her human spirit. The opposite is also true. You want to be miserable? Just coast through life folding at challenges and making excuses. "That's life, right?" Fuck that. Life is what you make of it, and so my mantra is "Mediocrity is the coward's path." I mean, seriously, how can you ever expect to have peace of mind when there's a constant gnawing inside you to tap into your infinite potential, but you half-ass it every step of the way?

All the hardships along my road have been there to teach me what I needed at that particular moment. Bottom line lesson: get your shit done. I can truly say I would not change one thing if I had to do it over again. It's all a matter of perspective; what I initially thought were setbacks were in truth blessings. In retrospect I'm thankful for everything I've been through. Those lessons humbled me tremendously. They made me realize that I still have a long way to go, but as long as I'm willing to fight the good fight every day and slug it out with my Enemy Mind, I'll get there.

Above All Else

The key is, find something that truly makes you happy and have fun with it.

The truth is, if you aren't enjoying something, you'll eventually give it up. People who love what they do are some of the most positive people I know. When you have a passion for the activity, you'll push through even when it's difficult. And you'll strive for perfection in it until you find a deeply honest inner joy and PMA. You can't separate heat and light from fire and still have fire, so PMA and inner joy are similarly inseparable.

Two questions: What are *you* here to do? What's your dharma, your soul's calling? What are your hopes and dreams? Your higher cause? Your purpose? Then: How will you wake up today and go after it?

I truly hope with all my heart and soul that what you've read in *The PMA Effect* will help you attain all that you desire and that you will pay it forward. If we work collectively, we can quickly turn things around on this planet. Let's be all in together. And let's keep up that PMA!

Thanks you for your time—your friend in service, John Joseph

Don't care what they may say. We got that attitude. Don't care what they may do. We got that attitude. Hey ... we got that PMA! Hey ... we got that PMA!

— Bad Brains, "Attitude"

Anyone desiring a 'FREE' download of A.C. Bhaktivedanta Swami Prabhupada's original translations of the beautiful Vedic literature please find them here.

https://bhaktivedantavediclibrary.org/

Acknowledgments

A.C. Bhaktivedanta Swami Prabhupada, Mom, Brahmabhuta Das, Vani Devi Das, E, Frank Sr., Blaise, Erika, Steve Reddy (Saci), Kate Reddy (Keli), Rich Roll, Julie (Srimati), Todd/Jen Irwin and the Boys, Tal and the Crossroads Crew, Aaron Drogoszewski, Artie Mac, Madman Jake, Karina, Bleu, Eileen, Bryan & Vickie Callen, Shaun/Kat Fowler, Peter Nussbaum, Jerri Mitchener, Krsna Bhakta, Ian Norrington, Ken Rideout, Rob Mohr, Bad Brains - HR, Doc, Darryl, Earl, The Artice Fam, Patty Jenkins, Sam Sheridan, Dan (ICM), Brian Wendel, Darshana, Orion Mims, Larry 'Rude-Boy' Wallach, Chris Garver, Toby, Moon & Max, Brendan Brazier, Jay Dublee RIP, Jimmy Brady, Joy, Bart and Benay (Candle Crew), Vlad & Fam (Organic Grill), Rick Richey, Marc (Recover NYC), Michael Alago, Paul DeGelder, Kim Graf, Todd Newman, Frank Grillo, Coach Samantha Murphy, Reece R., Kevin Custer, Ray Lego, Josh G (Clockwork BJJ), Bad Brains, Cro-Mags Fam (Craig Ahead, Mackie, AJ Novello),

Mike Dijan, Danny Diablo, Wisdom in Chains, Madball, AF, SOIA, Danny Schuler, Randy Blythe, Kip Anderson, Keegan, Mike Perrine, Pete Cervoni, Travis Barker, Jonathan Shaw, Scott Ebanks, Worldwide Hardcore Fam, Ironman Fam, Sids Bikes NYC, Delissa, Chris Skid, DMS Crew Worldwide, Bill Hall, Trevor Page, Loki, Howard & Arik (DSA) Victoria Moran, Tim Borer, Joey Castillo, Nick Oliveri, Brian Rose, Rip Esselstyn, Chad Sarno, Madi/Rose Serpico, Rickster, Gene Bauer, Scott Winegart, Dan (Canada), Loll Loleit, Vinny Signorelli, Ajay/Kittie and the James Gang, Doug Crosby, Dr. Robert Ostfeld, Angela Dumadag, Alexander Owens & The Owens Family, CTF Crew, Elgin James, Erica and Mike, Dan Ilchuk, Civ, Steve-O, Pete & Jackie Barber, Jesse Malin, Francis B., Badarayana Das, Max (Shogun), Jake Shields, Jamey Jasta, Knarly Gav Ink, Joe Hardcore, Mac Danzig, Moby, DMS Crew, Power/Saes & The NYC Bridgerunner Crew, Robin Arzon, Sam Cardona, Steve Lacy, STS, Todd Vance, Tony Kanal, Dr. Garth Davis, Dr. Joel Kahn, Overthrow Boxing NYC, Monkey Bar Gym, Dan Hardy, Chopper, Todd/Kimberly Morse, Dov Davidoff, Forty Deuce Radio, Mike Schnapp, David Carter, Mercy for Animals, Kevin McQuaide (RIP), Foose, Gary Holt, Molecule Water NYC, Big Walt McCormick, Crazy-Ass Jay (F.O.H.), The Cheeky Yam, Felt Bikes, Cuore Swiss Custom Kits, Felipe Rudy Project, Bob Kirkup, Philipp Styra & all those spreading the P.M.A. and fighting for the rights of the innocent in order to make this world a better place. Hari Bol!